FOR ORGANS, PIANOS & ELECTRONIC KEYBOARDS

E-Z PLAY® TODAY

287

JOSH GROBAN

T0082056

Cover photo by Christan Lantry

ISBN: 978-1-4234-4716-0

HAL•LEONARD®
CORPORATION

7777 W. BLUEMOUND RD. P.O. BOX 13819 MILWAUKEE, WI 53213

Visit Hal Leonard Online at
www.halleonard.com

Awake

Registration 4
Rhythm: 4/4 Ballad

Words and Music by Josh Groban,
Thomas Salter and Eric Mouquet

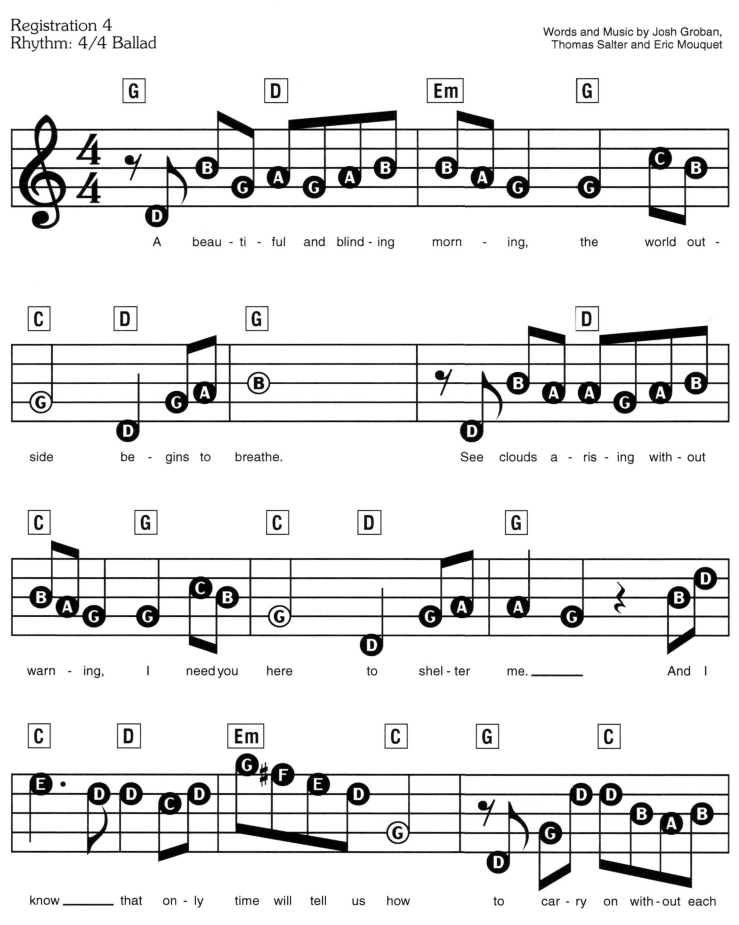

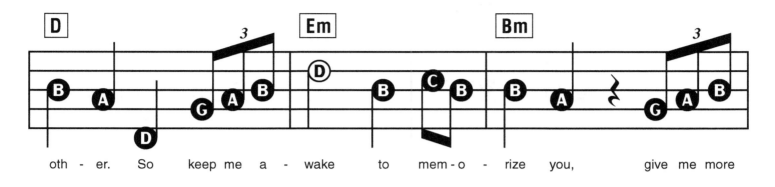

oth - er. So keep me a - wake to mem-o - rize you, give me more

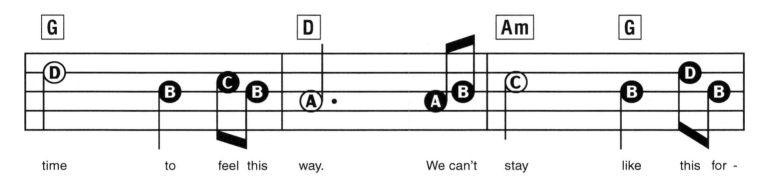

time to feel this way. We can't stay like this for -

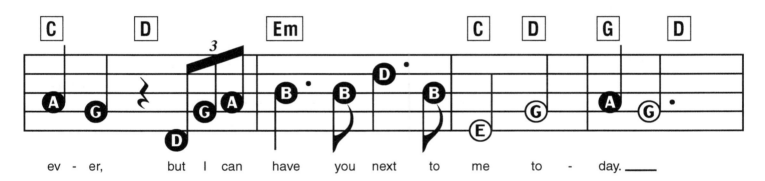

ev - er, but I can have you next to me to - day. _____

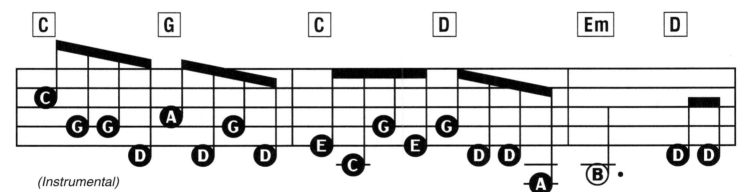

(Instrumental)

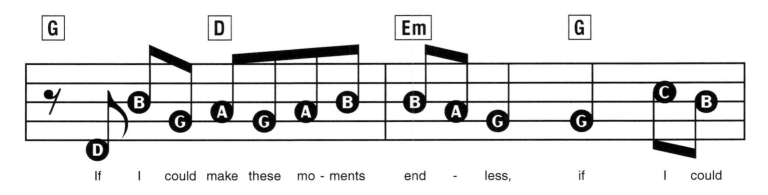

If I could make these mo - ments end - less, if I could

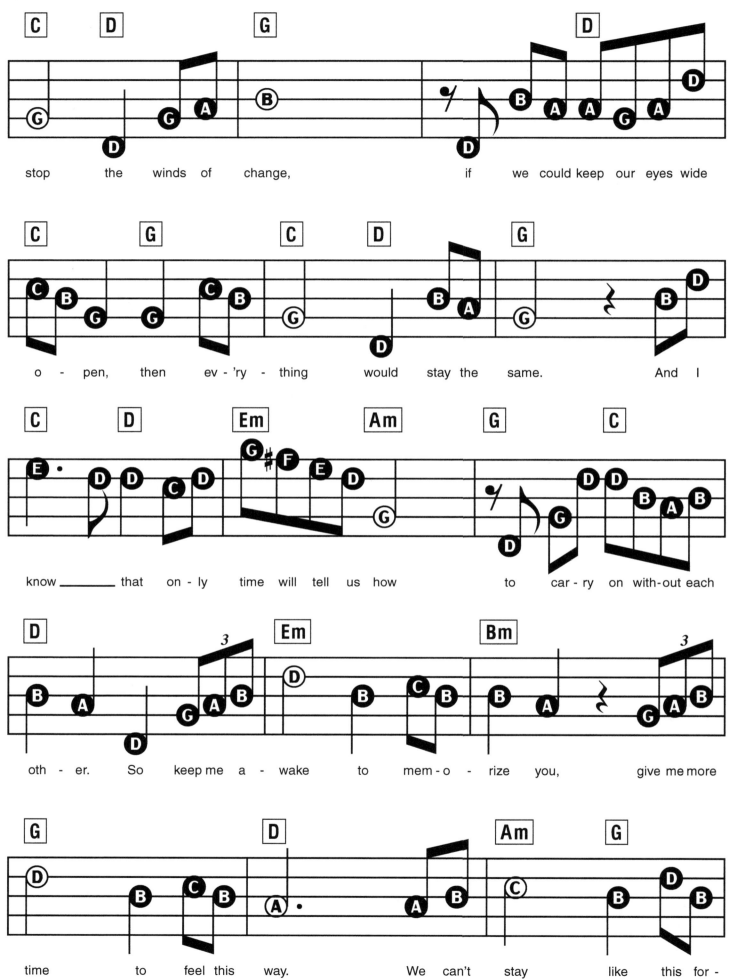

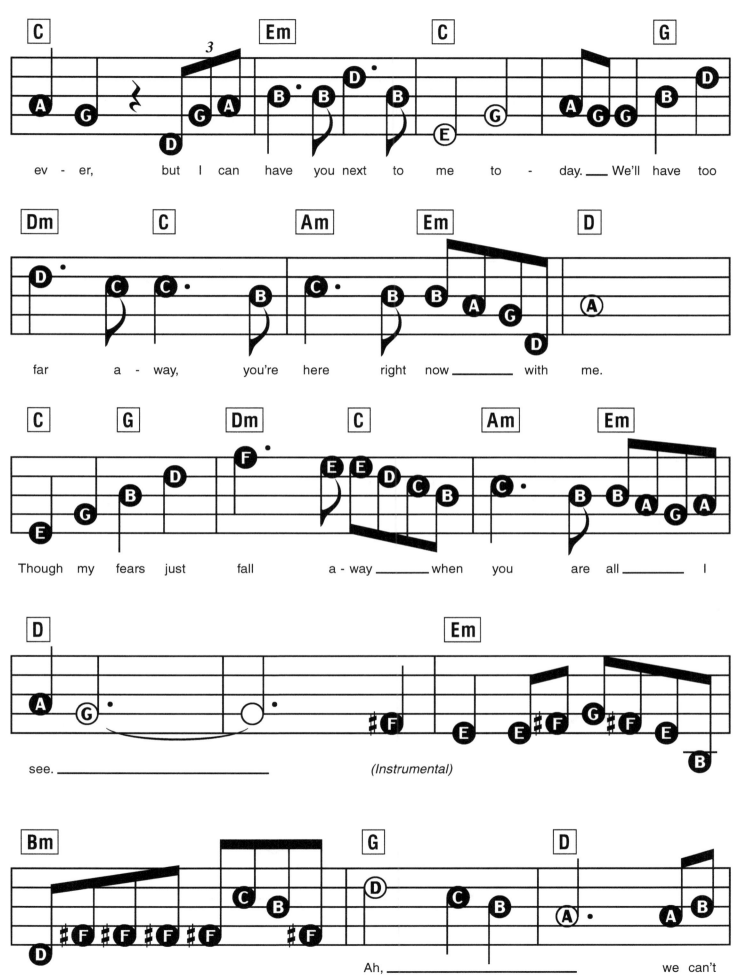

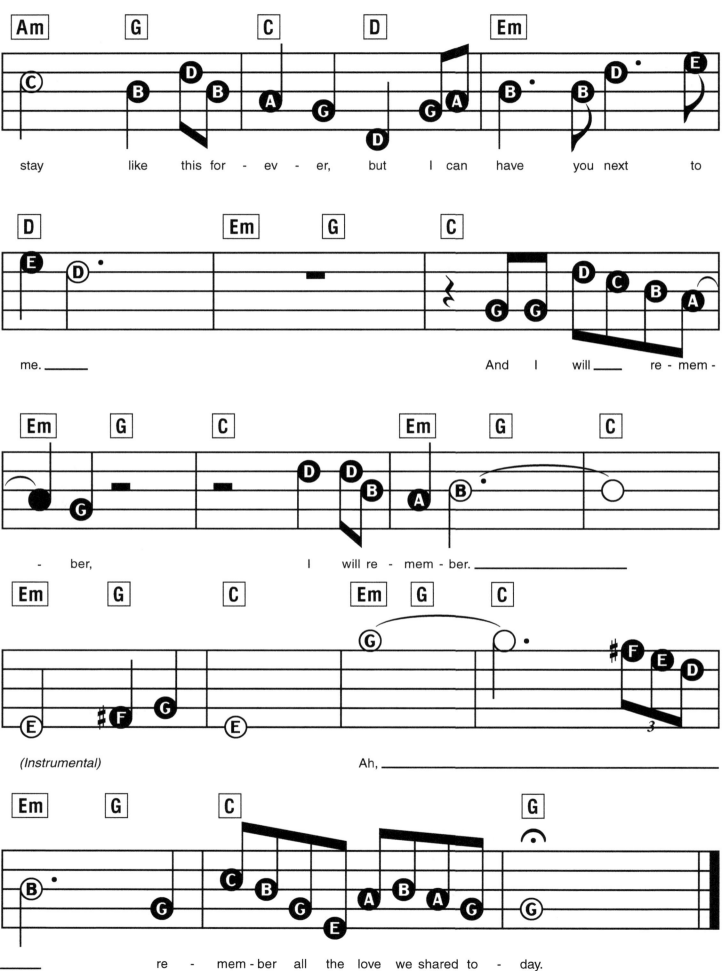

stay   like   this for - ev - er,   but   I   can   have   you   next   to

me. _____   And   I   will ___   re - mem -

- ber,   I   will re - mem - ber. _____

(Instrumental)   Ah, _____

_____   re - mem - ber   all   the   love   we   shared   to - day.

Believe
from Warner Bros. Pictures' THE POLAR EXPRESS

Registration 8
Rhythm: 4/4 Ballad

Words and Music by Glen Ballard
and Alan Silvestri

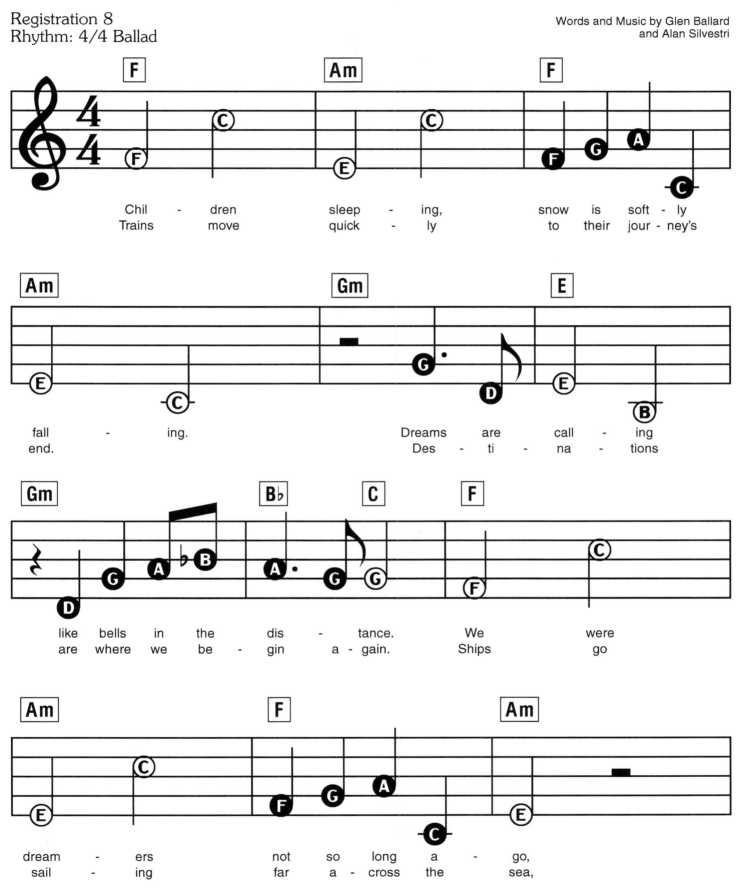

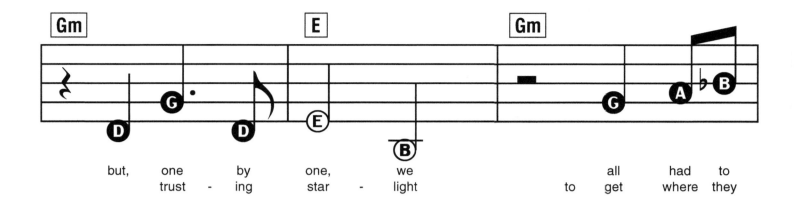

but, one by one, we all had to
trust - ing star - light to get where they

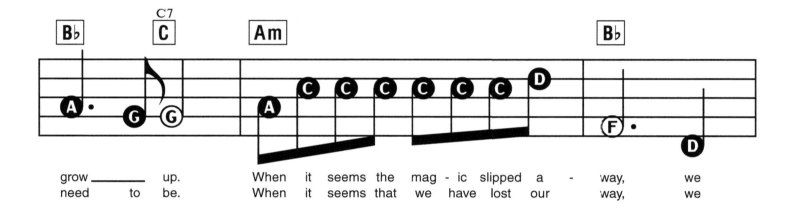

grow _____ up. When it seems the mag - ic slipped a - way, we
need to be. When it seems that we have lost our way, we

To Coda ⊕

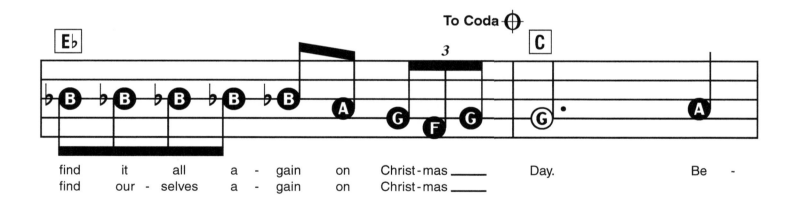

find it all a - gain on Christ - mas _____ Day. Be -
find our - selves a - gain on Christ - mas _____

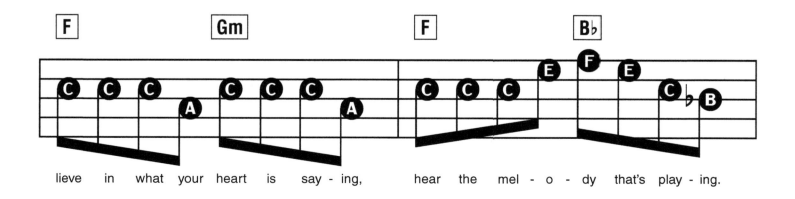

lieve in what your heart is say - ing, hear the mel - o - dy that's play - ing.

Canto Alla Vita

Registration 4
Rhythm: 8 Beat or Rock

Words and Music by Giuseppe Dettori,
Antonio Galbiati and Alfredo Rapetti

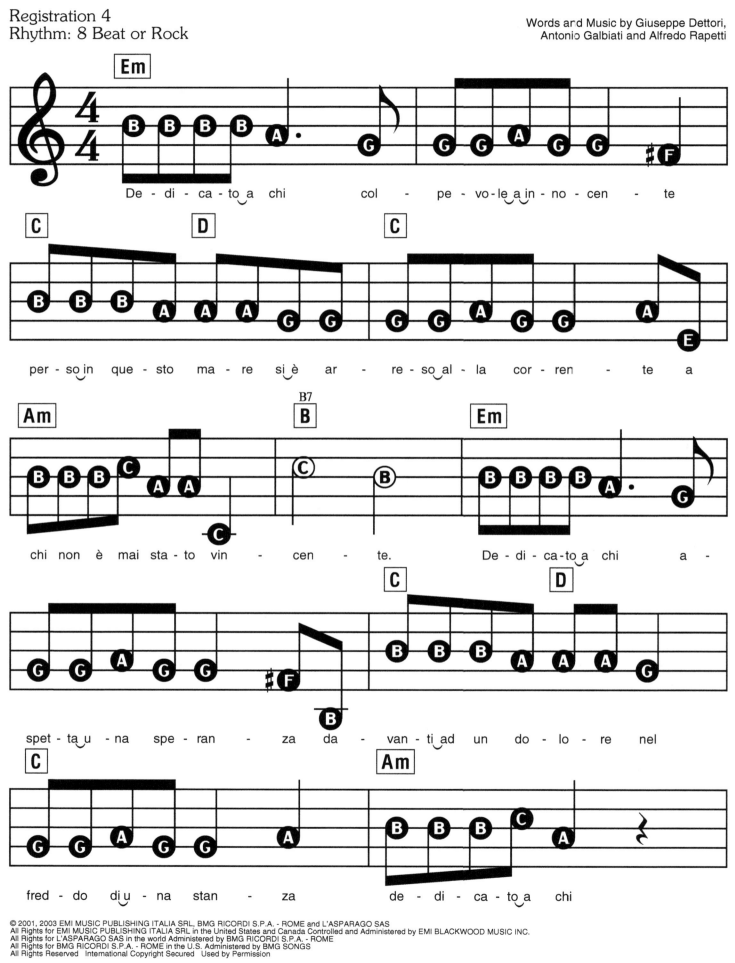

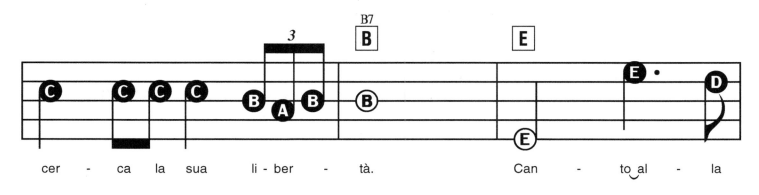

cer - ca la sua li - ber - tà. Can - to al - la

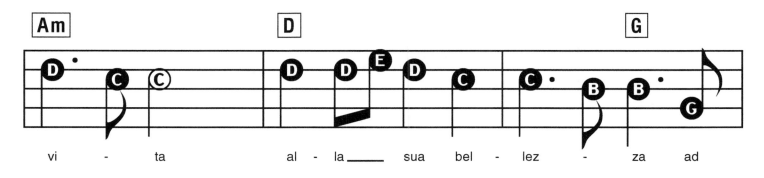

vi - ta al - la_____ sua bel - lez - za ad

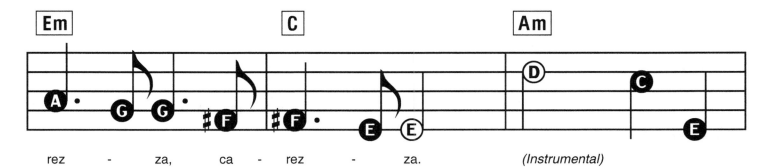

o - gni sua fe - ri - ta o - gni____ sua ca -

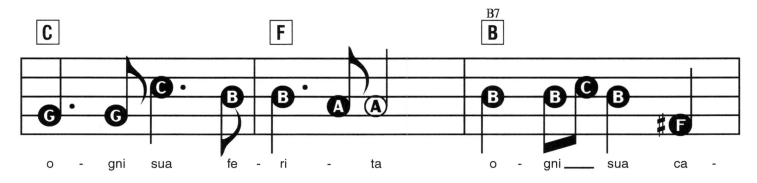

rez - za, ca - rez - za. *(Instrumental)*

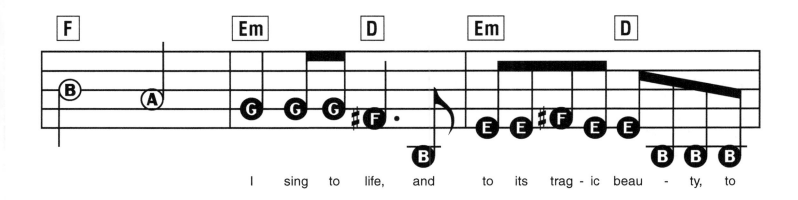

I sing to life, and to its trag - ic beau - ty, to

14

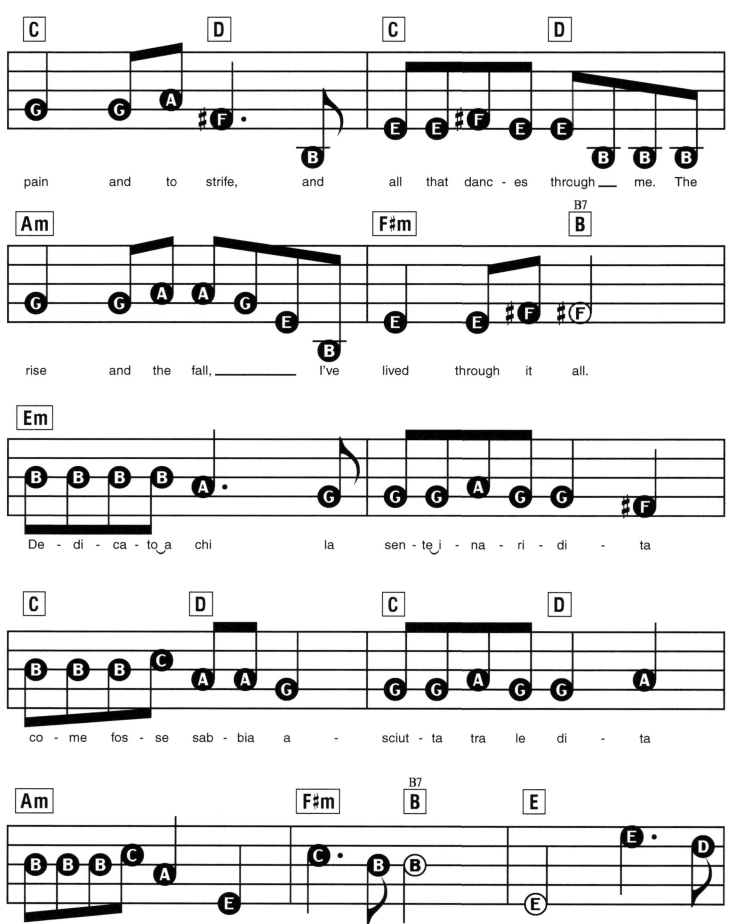

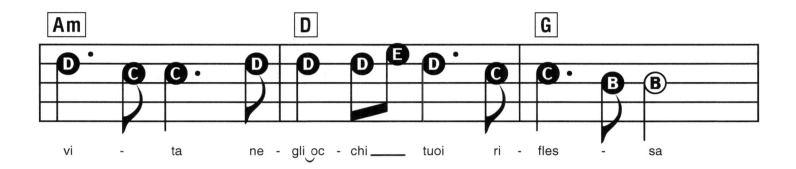

vi - ta ne - gli oc - chi___ tuoi ri - fles - sa

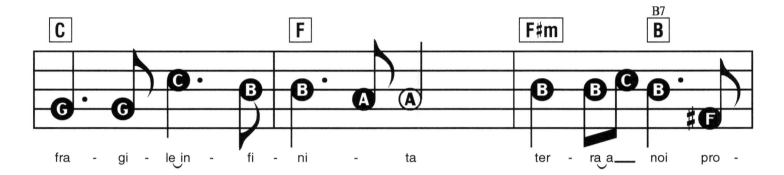

fra - gi - le in - fi - ni - ta ter - ra a___ noi pro -

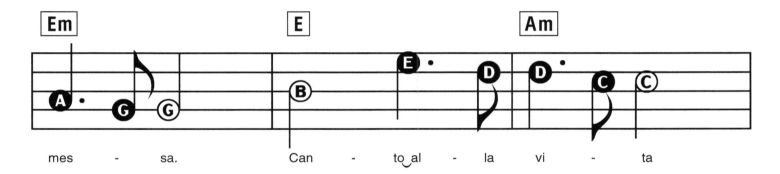

mes - sa. Can - to al - la vi - ta

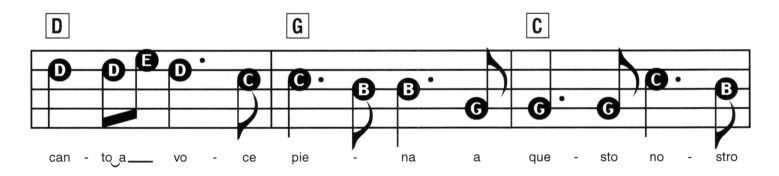

can - to a___ vo - ce pie - na a que - sto no - stro

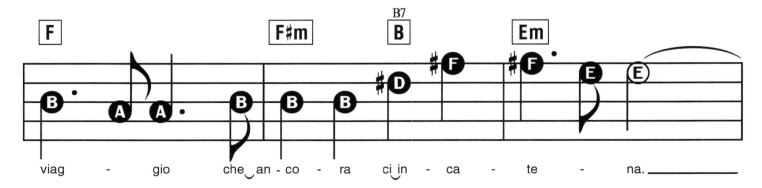

viag - gio che an - co - ra ci in - ca - te - na.___

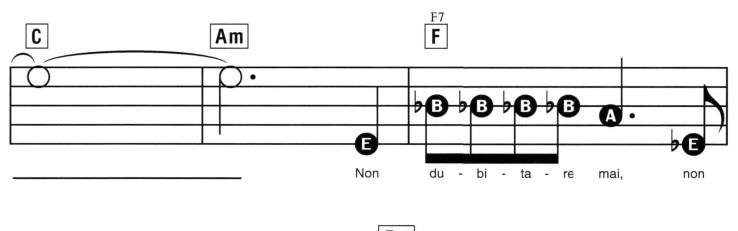

Non du - bi - ta - re mai, non

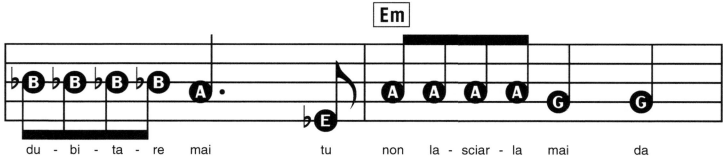

du - bi - ta - re mai tu non la - sciar - la mai da

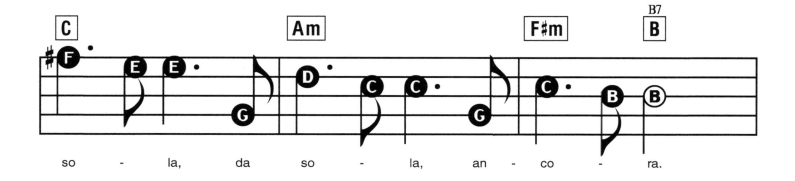

so - la, da so - la, an - co - ra.

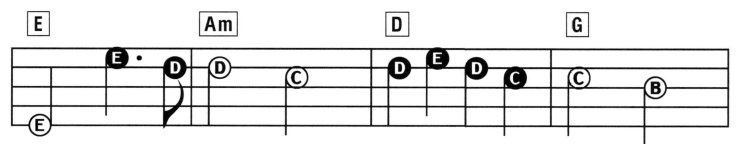

(Instrumental)

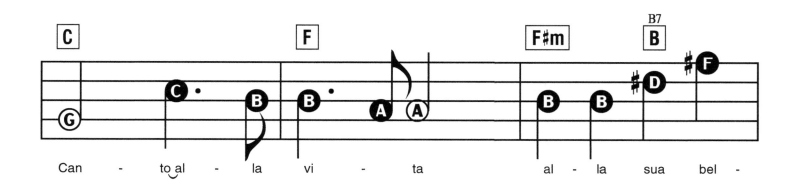

Can - to al - la vi - ta al - la sua bel -

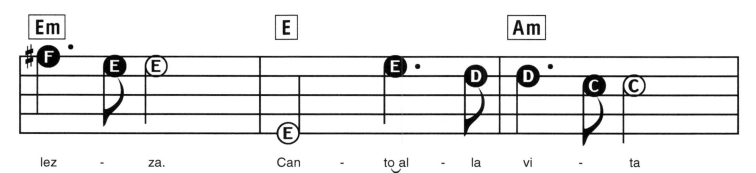

lez - za. Can - to al - la vi - ta

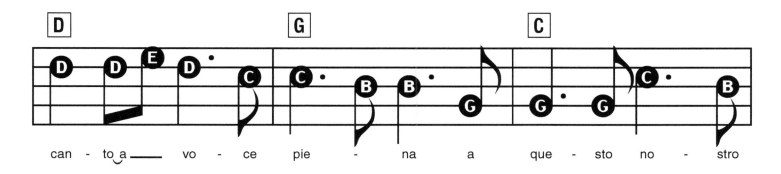

can - to a ___ vo - ce pie - na a que - sto no - stro

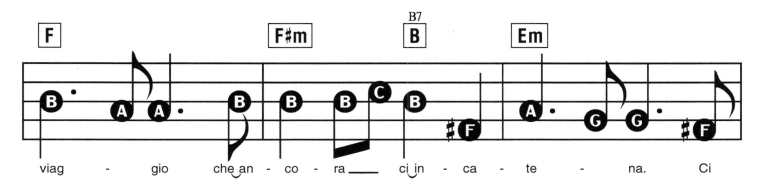

viag - gio che an - co - ra ___ ci in - ca - te - na. Ci

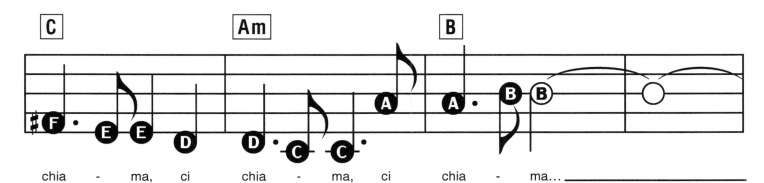

chia - ma, ci chia - ma, ci chia - ma... ___

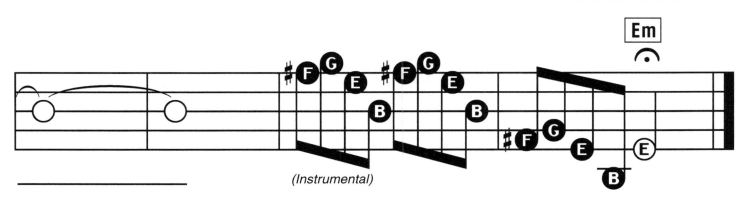

___ *(Instrumental)*

February Song

Registration 8
Rhythm: Waltz

Words by John Ondrasik and Josh Groban
Music by Josh Groban and Marius De Vries

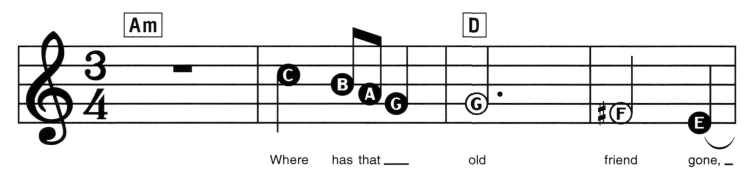

Where has that ___ old friend gone, ___

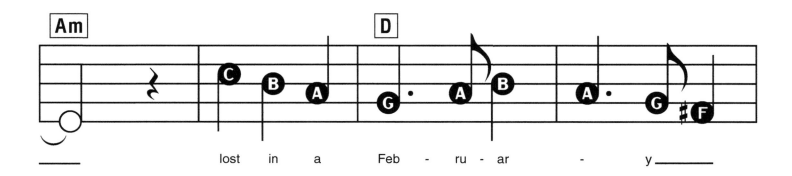

___ lost in a Feb - ru - ar - y _____

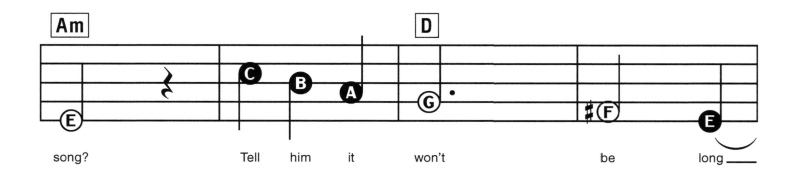

song? Tell him it won't be long ___

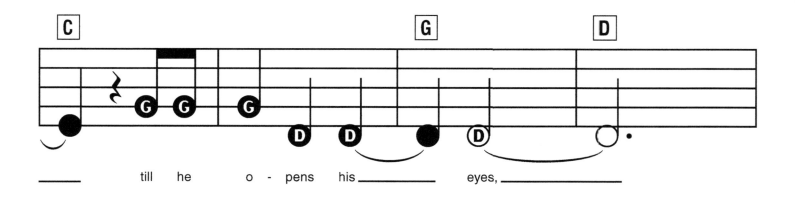

___ till he o - pens his _____ eyes, _____

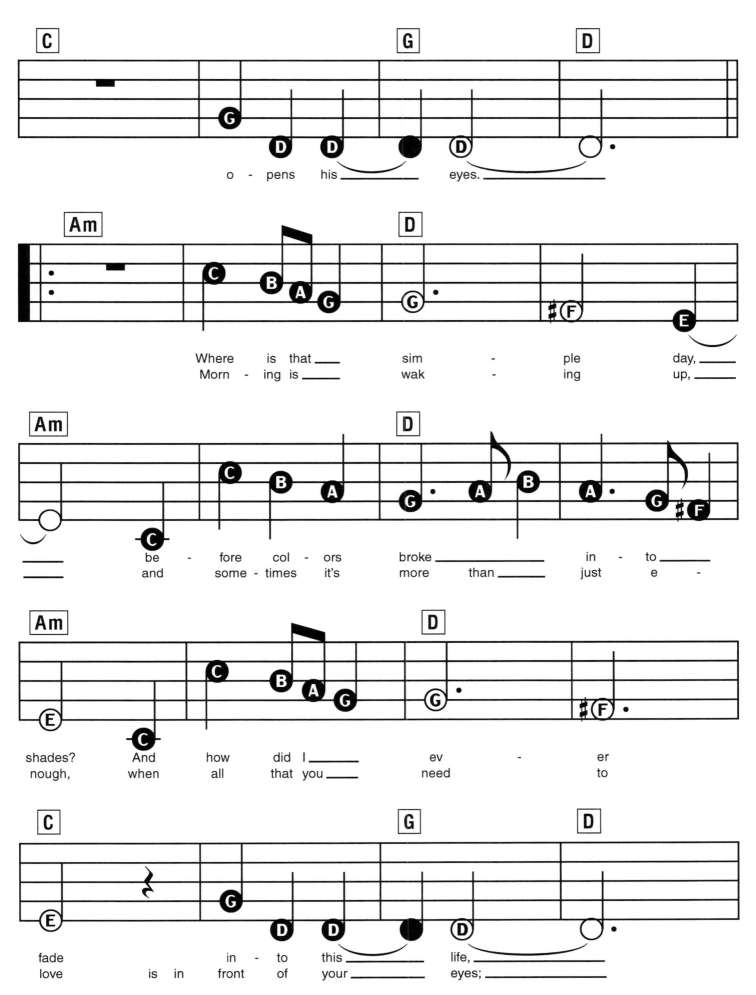

20

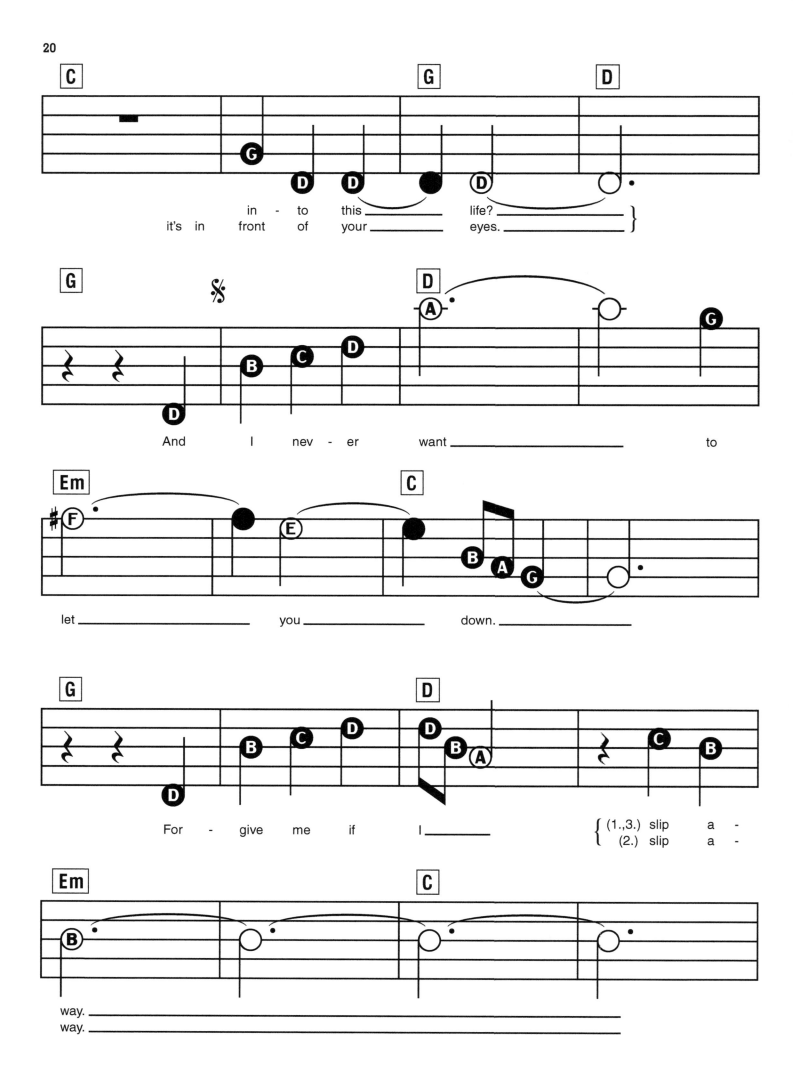

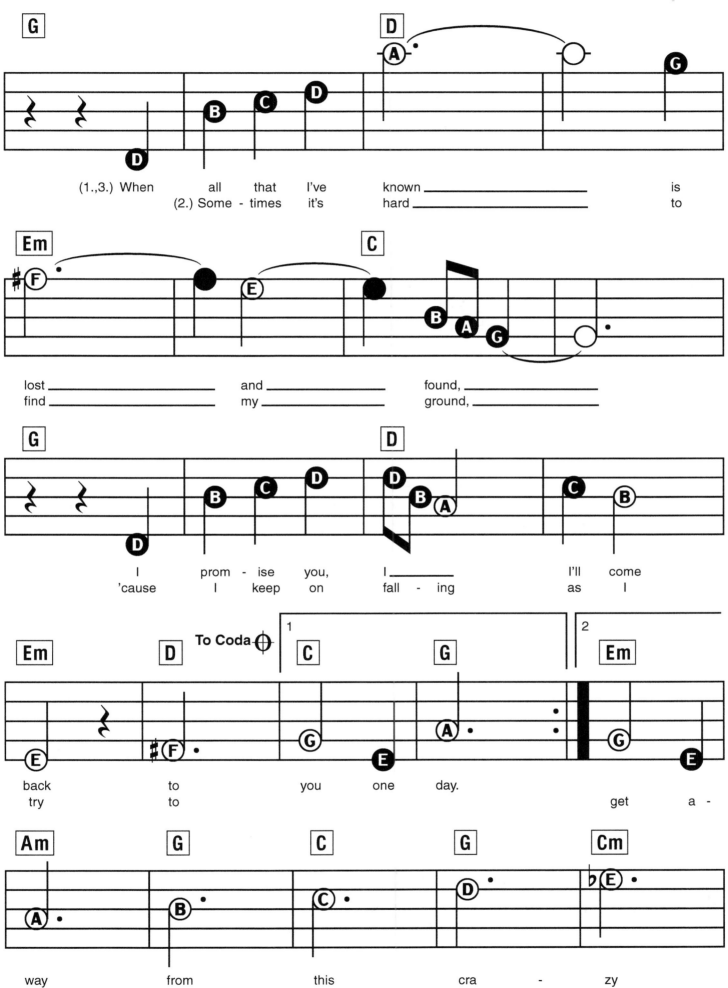

(1.,3.) When all that I've known _____ is
(2.) Some - times it's hard _____ to

lost _____ and _____ found, _____
find _____ my _____ ground, _____

I prom - ise you, I _____ I'll come
'cause I keep on fall - ing as I

back to you one day.
try to get a -

way from this cra - zy

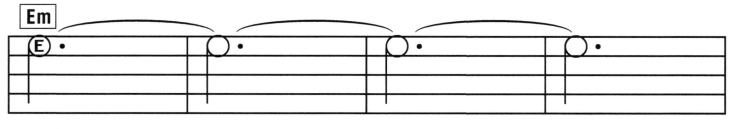

world.

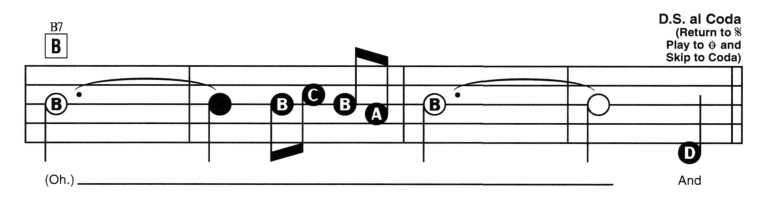

D.S. al Coda
(Return to %
Play to ⊕ and
Skip to Coda)

(Oh.) _____ And

CODA ⊕

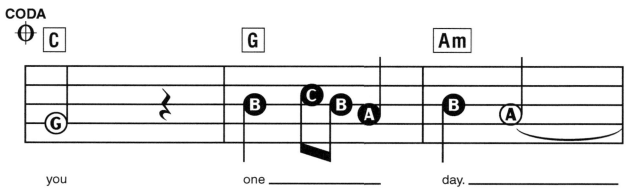

you   one _____   day. _____

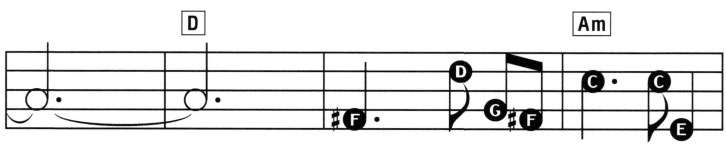

(Instrumental)

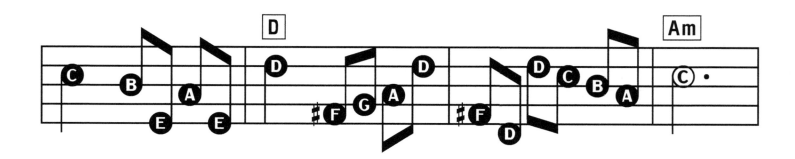

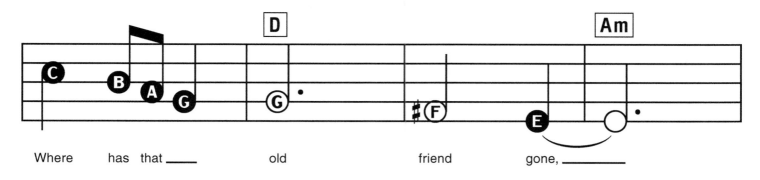

Where has that ___ old friend gone, ___

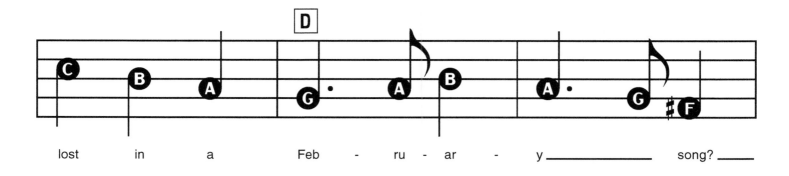

lost in a Feb - ru - ar - y ___ song? ___

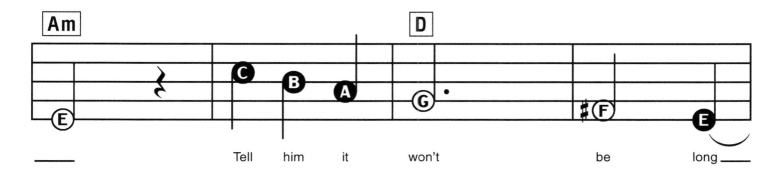

___ Tell him it won't be long ___

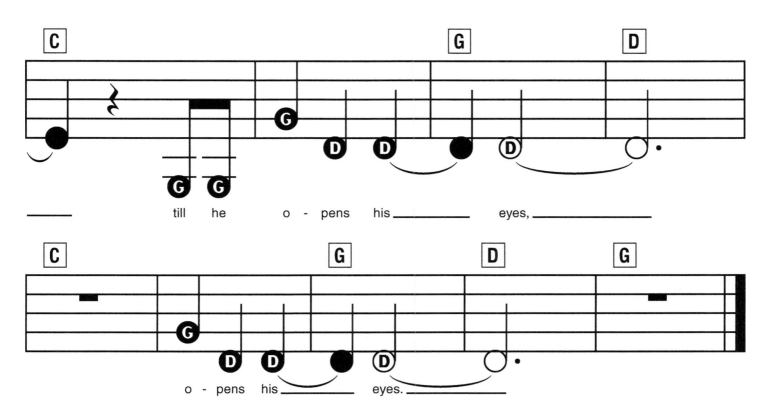

___ till he o - pens his ___ eyes, ___

o - pens his ___ eyes. ___

Gira Con Me

Registration 8
Rhythm: None

Words and Music by Walter Afanasieff,
David Foster and Lucio Quarantotto

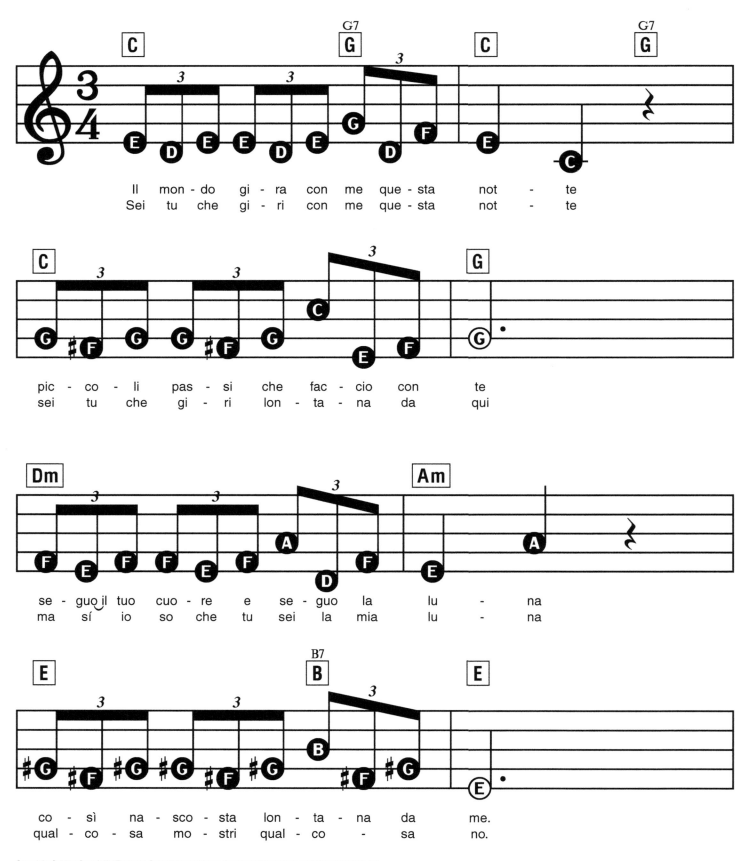

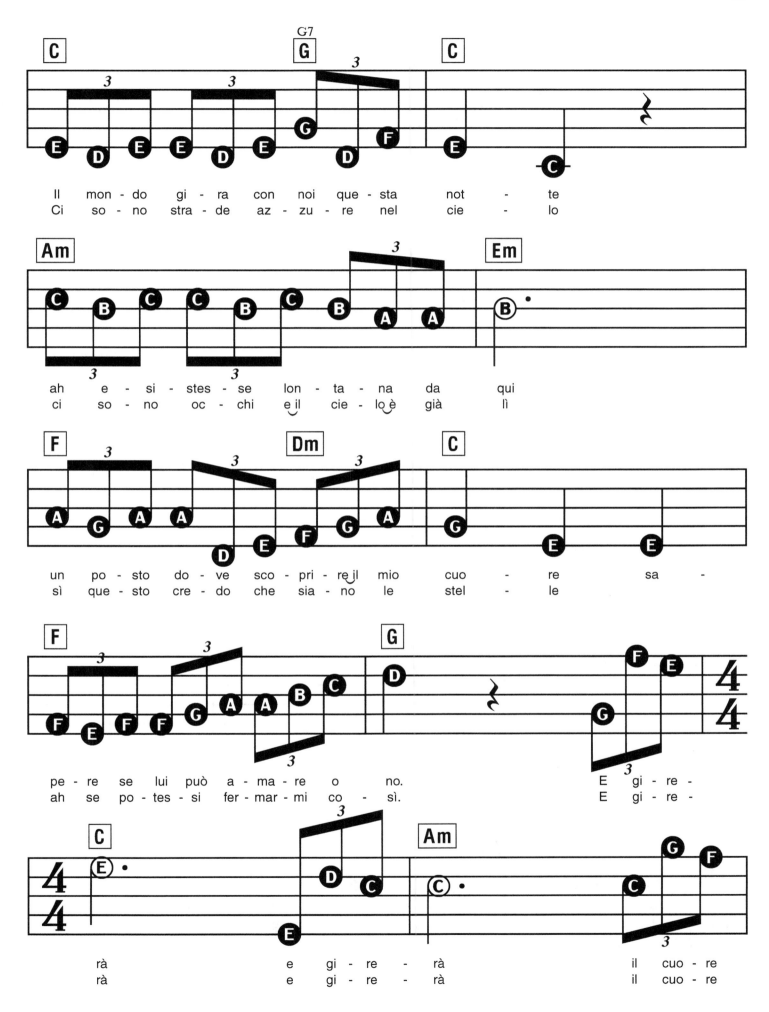

(Instrumental)

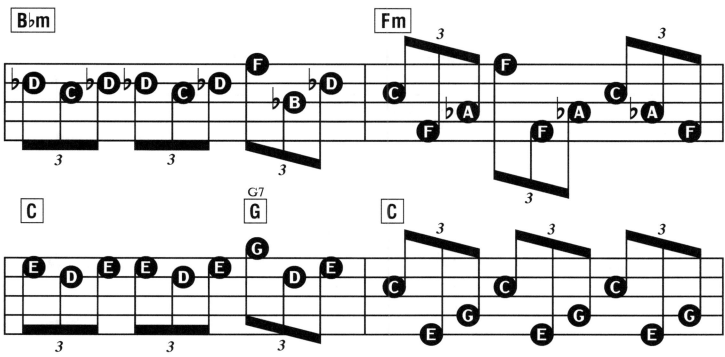

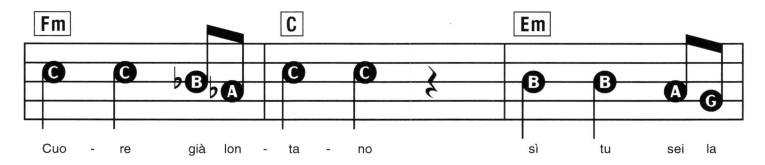

Cuo - re già lon - ta - no   sì   tu   sei   la

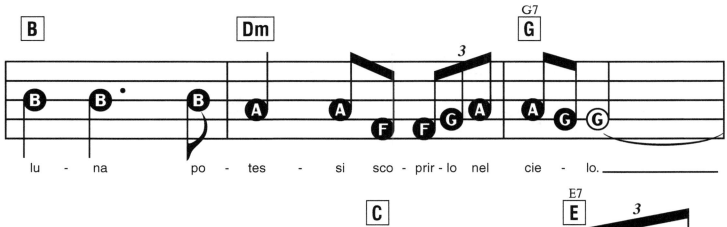

lu - na   po - tes - si   sco - prir - lo   nel   cie - lo._____

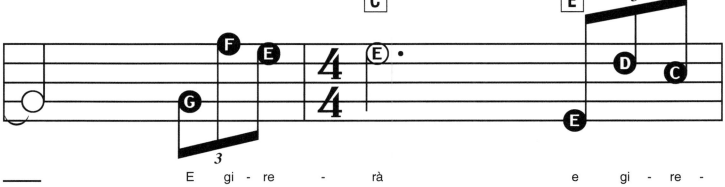

_____   E   gi - re - rà   e   gi - re -

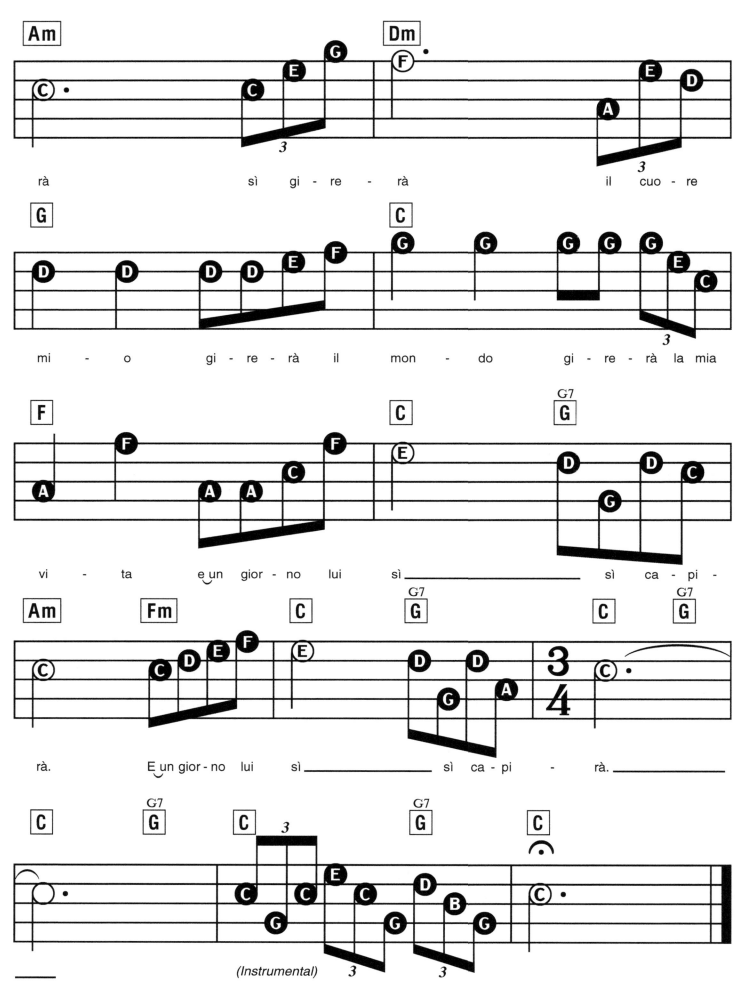

rà   sì gi - re - rà   il cuo - re

mi - o gi - re - rà il mon - do gi - re - rà la mia

vi - ta e un gior - no lui sì _____ sì ca - pi -

rà.   E un gior - no lui sì _____ sì ca - pi - rà. _____

_____   (Instrumental)

In Her Eyes

Registration 1
Rhythm: None

Lyrics by Michael Ochs and Jeff Cohen
Music by Michael Ochs, Jeff Cohen and Andy Selby

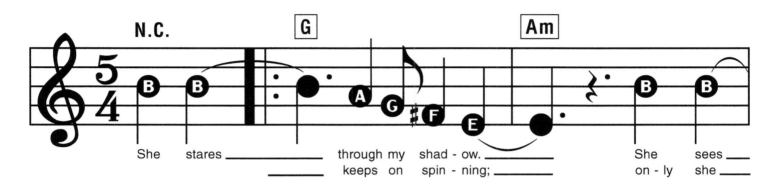

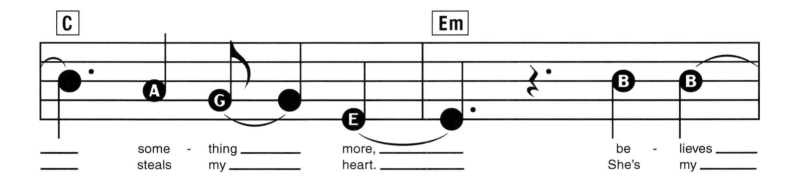

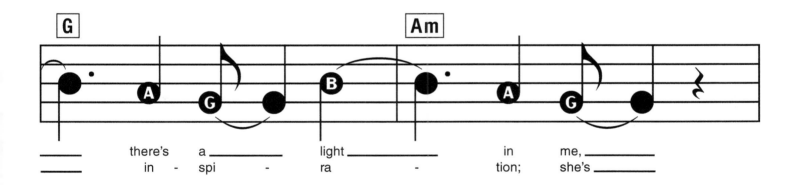

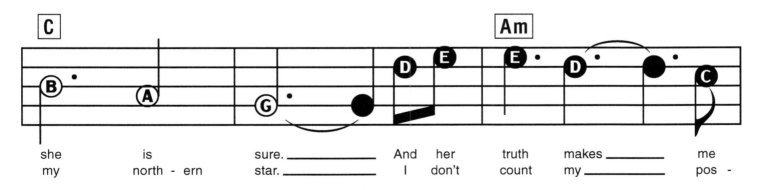

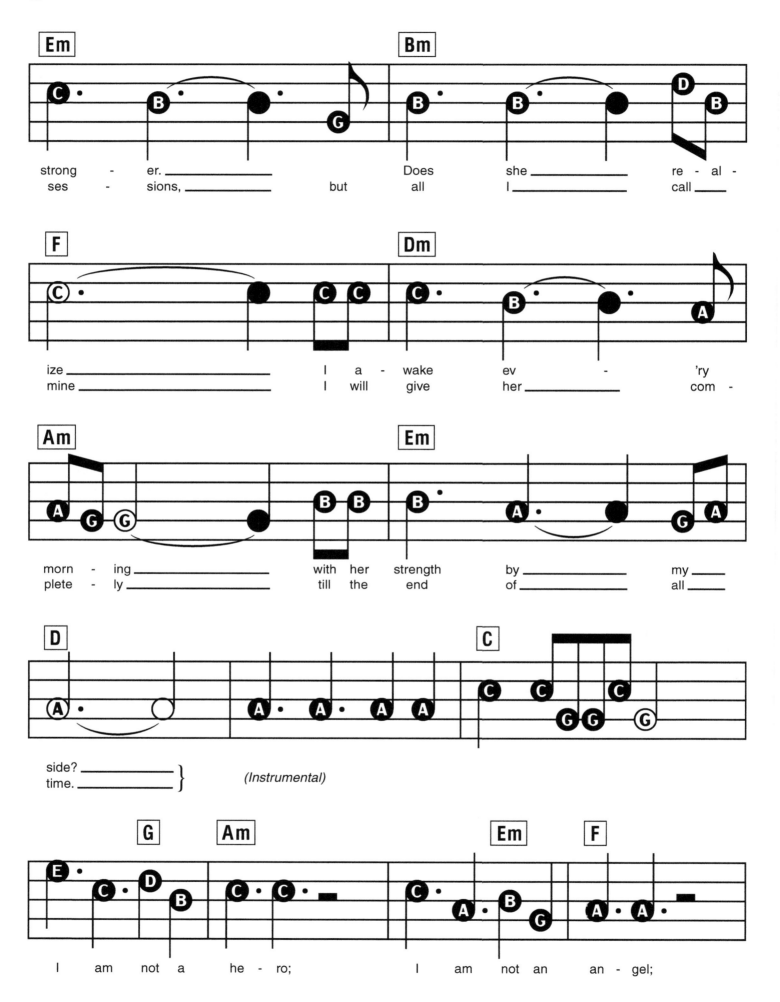

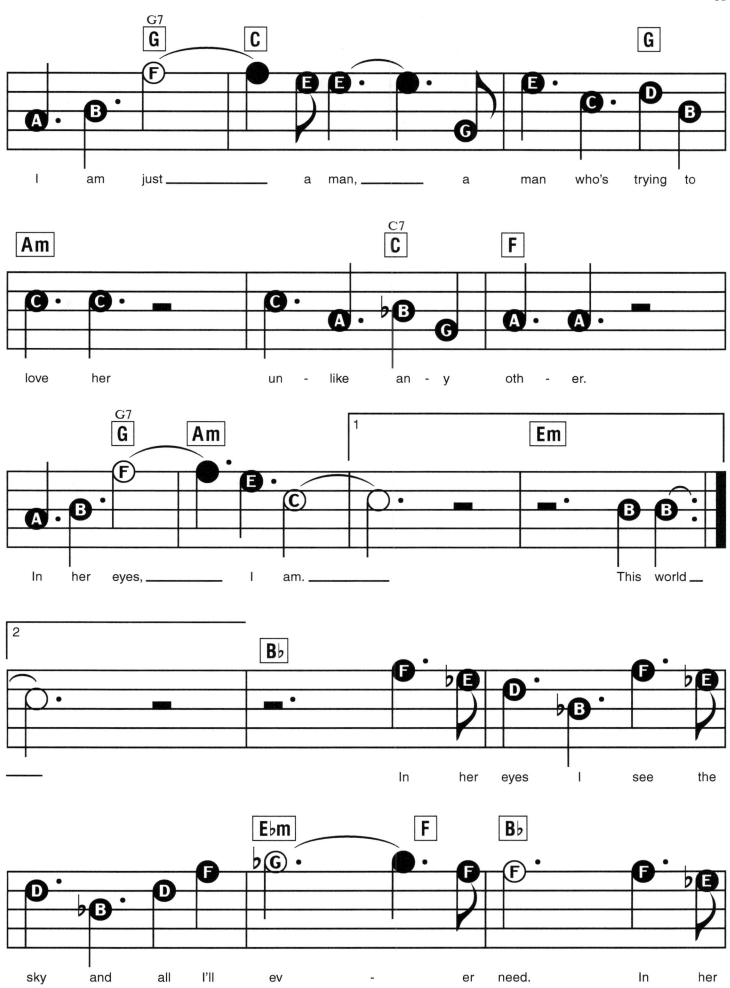

32

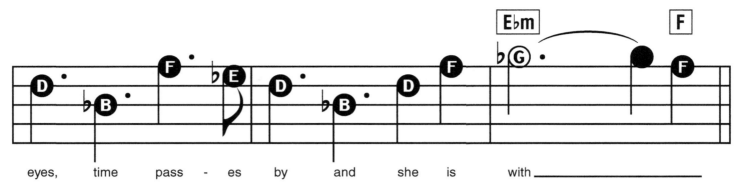

eyes,   time   pass - es   by   and   she   is   with _____

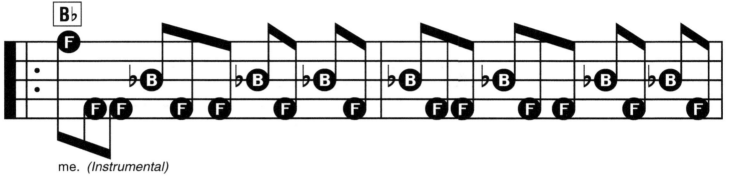

me. *(Instrumental)*
(Vocal 1st time only)

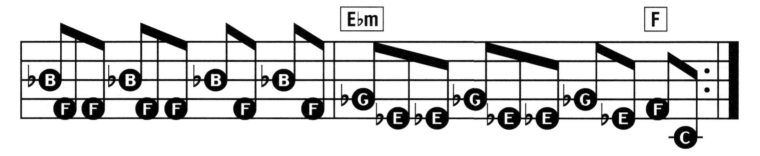

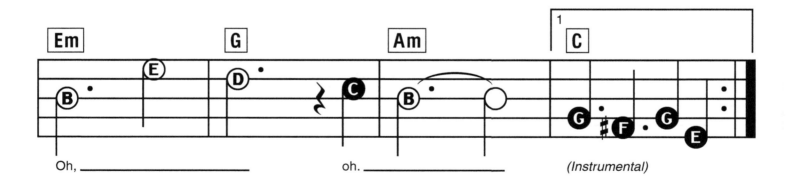

Oh, _____   oh. _____   *(Instrumental)*

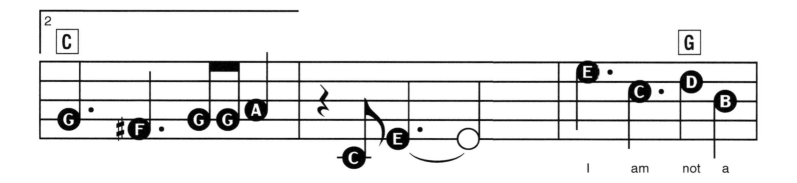

I   am   not   a

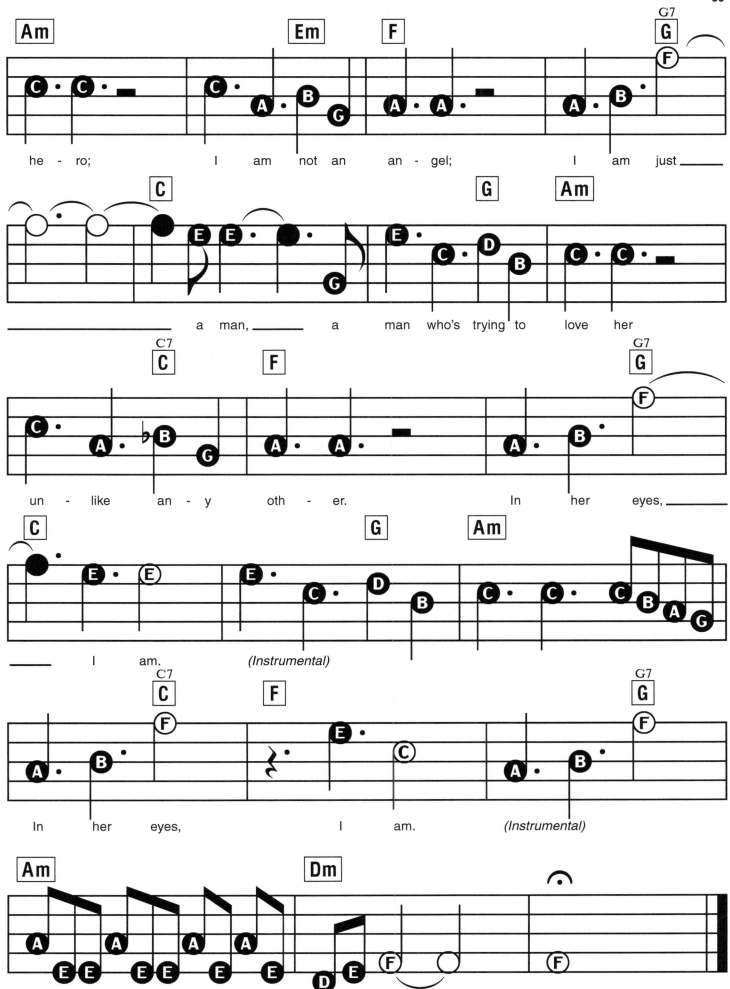

Never Let Go

Registration 3
Rhythm: 8 Beat or Rock

Words and Music by Eric Mouquet
and Josh Groban

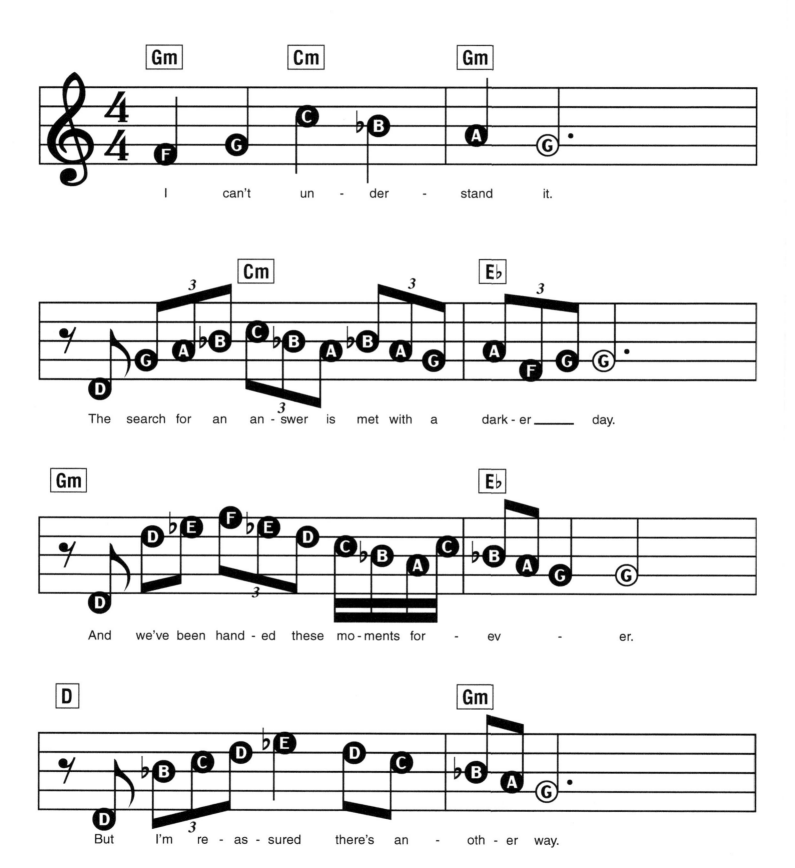

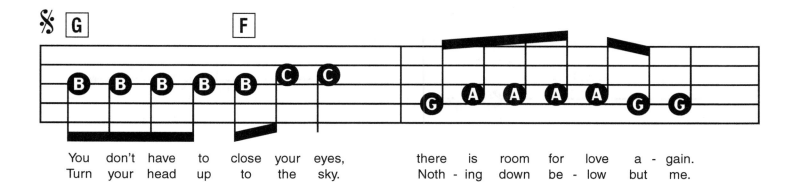

You don't have to close your eyes, there is room for love a - gain.
Turn your head up to the sky. Noth - ing down be - low but me.

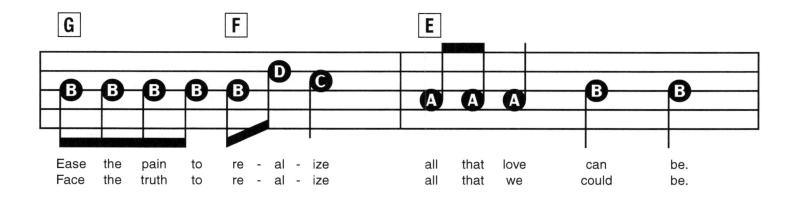

Ease the pain to re - al - ize all that love can be.
Face the truth to re - al - ize all that we could be.

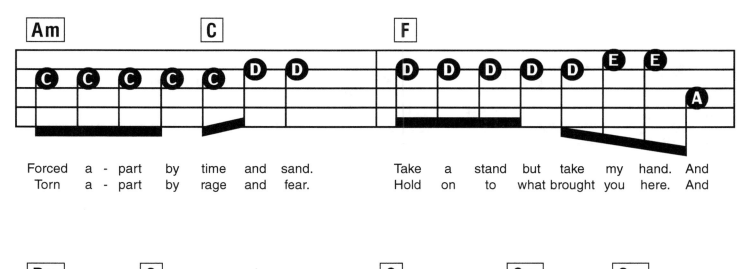

Forced a - part by time and sand. Take a stand but take my hand. And
Torn a - part by rage and fear. Hold on to what brought you here. And

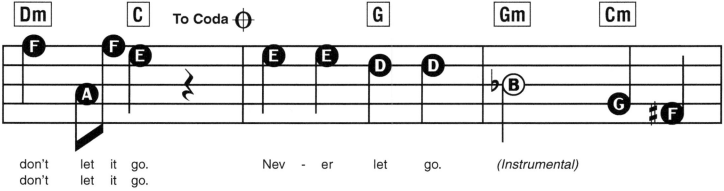

To Coda

don't let it go. Nev - er let go. (Instrumental)
don't let it go.

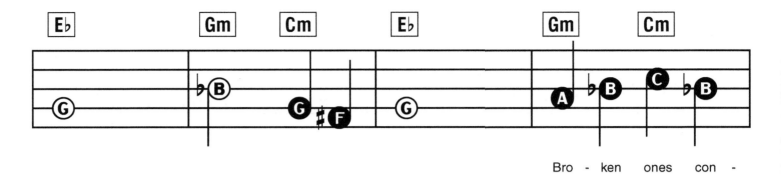

Bro - ken ones con -

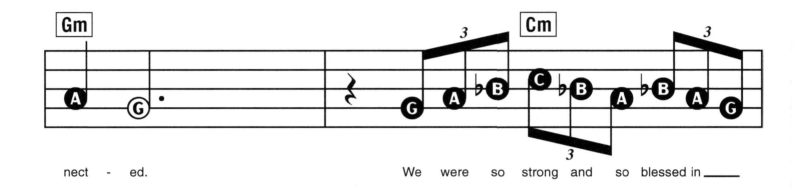

nect - ed.   We   were   so   strong   and   so   blessed in ____

D.S. al Coda
(Return to 𝄉
Play to ⊕ and
Skip to Coda)

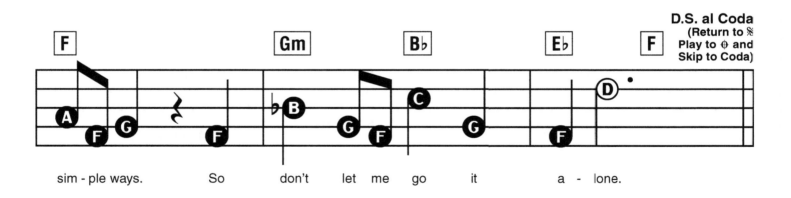

sim - ple ways.   So   don't   let   me   go   it   a - lone.

CODA

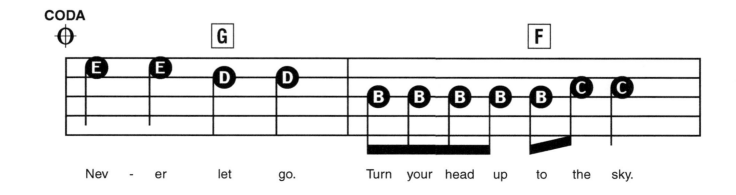

Nev - er   let   go.   Turn   your   head   up   to   the   sky.

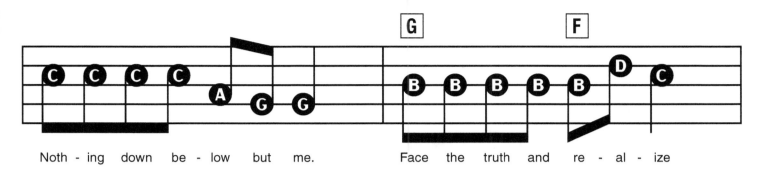

Noth - ing down be - low but me. Face the truth and re - al - ize

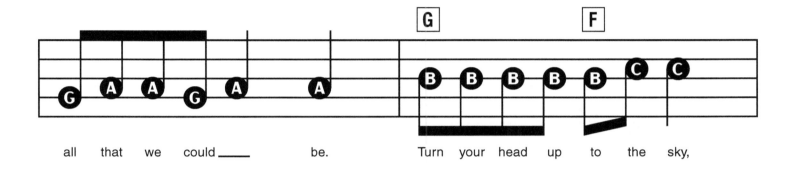

all that we could ___ be. Turn your head up to the sky,

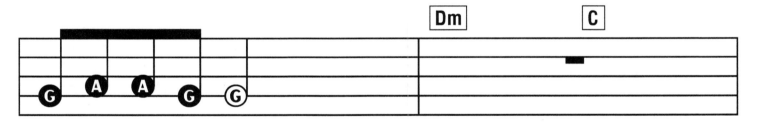

noth - ing down be - low.

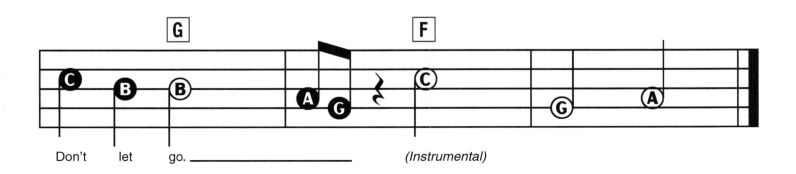

Don't let go. _____ (Instrumental)

Now or Never

Registration 4
Rhythm: Ballad or 8 Beat

Words and Music by Josh Groban
and Imogen Heap

| Dm | F | B♭ | F |

I watched the morn - ing dawn up - on your skin,
Sweep - ing egg - shells still at three a. - m.:

| Dm | F | B♭ | F |

a splin - ter in the light.
we're try - ing far too hard,

| Dm | F | B♭ | F |

It caught and frayed the ver - y heart of us. It's been
the tat - tered thought bal - loons a - bove our heads sink - ing

| Dm | F | B♭ | F |

hid - ing there in - side for all this time.
in the weight of all we need to say.

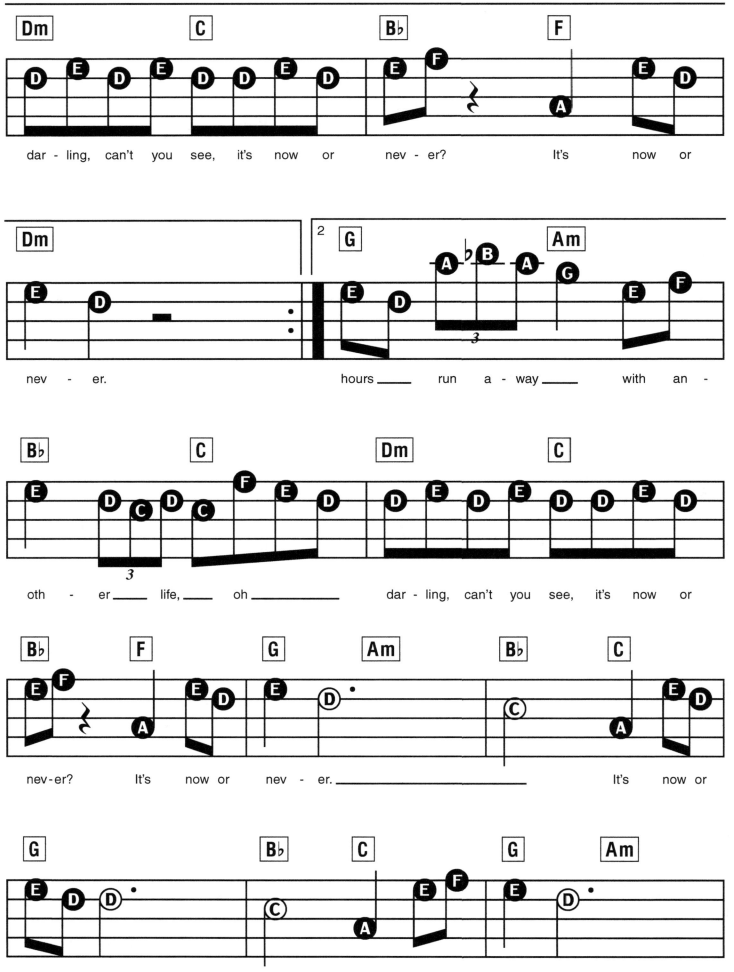

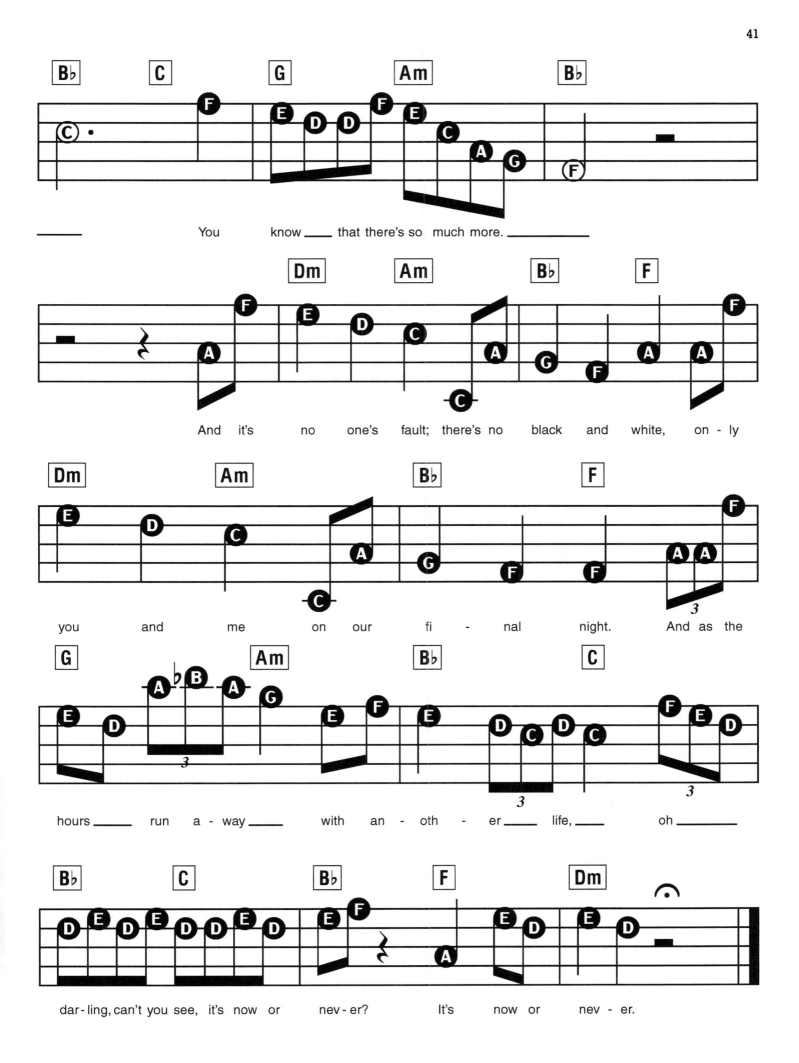

Per Te

Registration 4
Rhythm: 4/4 Ballad

Music by Walter Afanasieff and Josh Groban
Lyrics by Marco Marinangeli

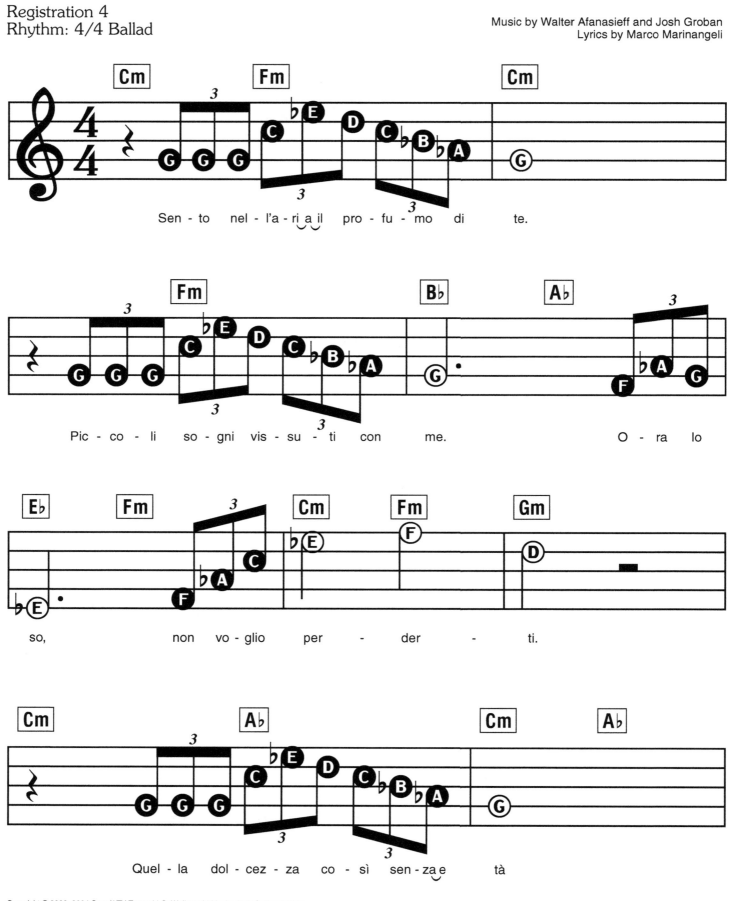

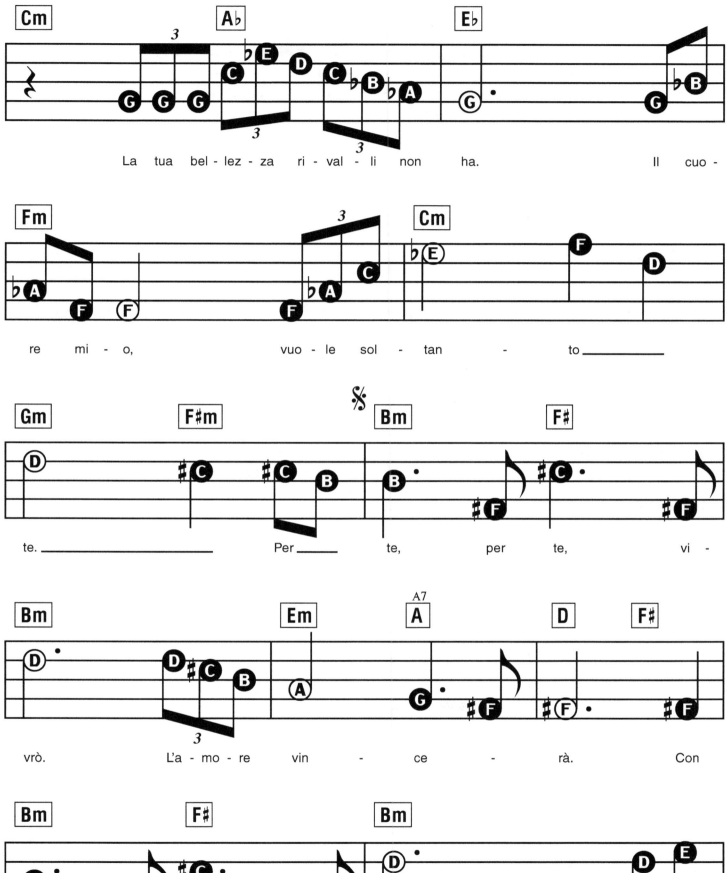

La tua bel - lez - za ri - val - li non ha. Il cuo -

re mi - o, vuo - le sol - tan - to _____

te. _____ Per ____ te, per te, vi -

vrò. L'a - mo - re vin - ce - rà. Con

te, con te, av - rò. Mil - le

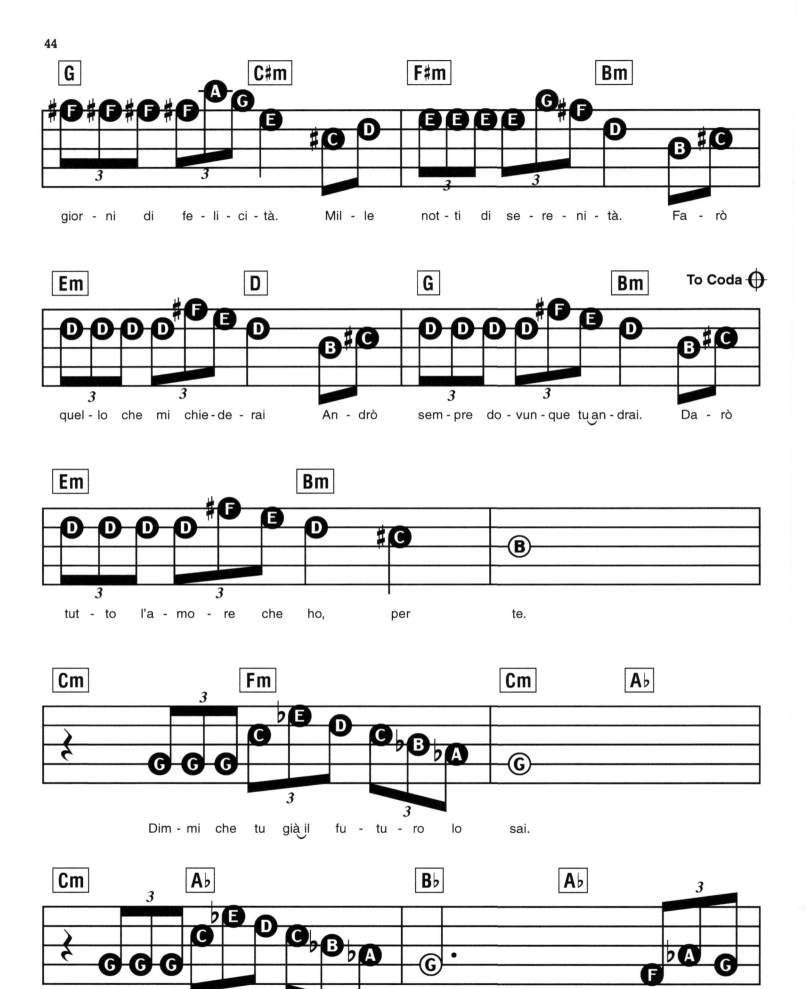

D.S. al Coda
(Return to ℅
Play to ⊕ and
Skip to Coda)

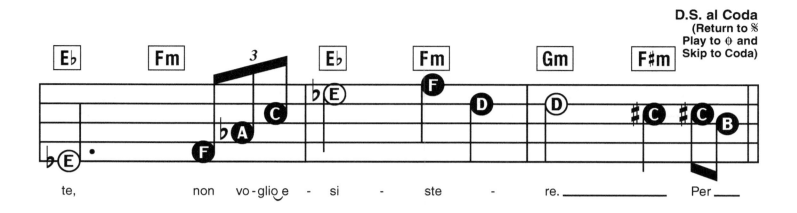

te, non vo-glio e - si - ste - re. _____ Per ___

CODA

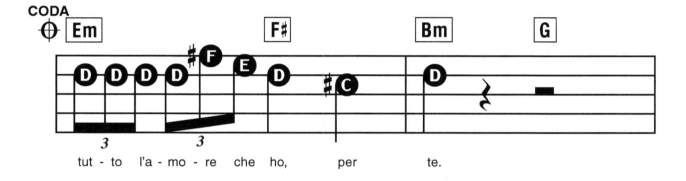

tut - to l'a - mo - re che ho, per te.

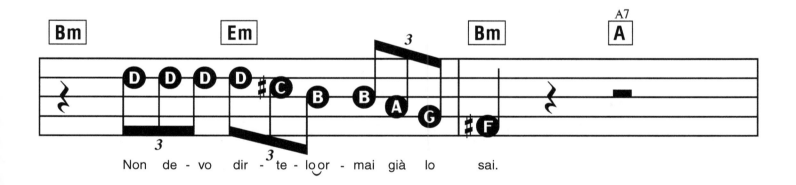

Non de - vo dir - te - lo or - mai già lo sai.

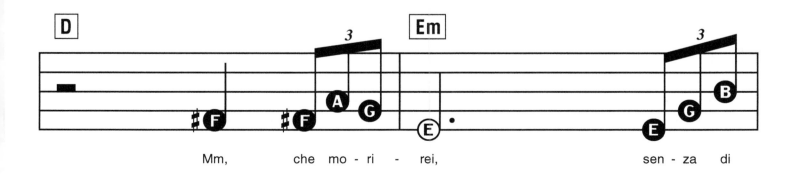

Mm, che mo - ri - rei, sen - za di

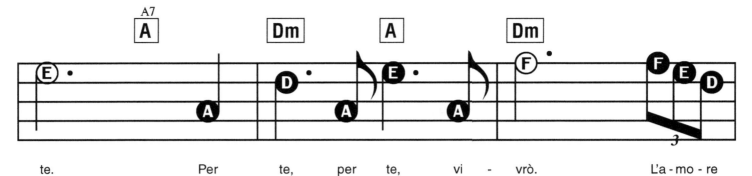

te.   Per   te,   per   te,   vi - vrò.   L'a - mo - re

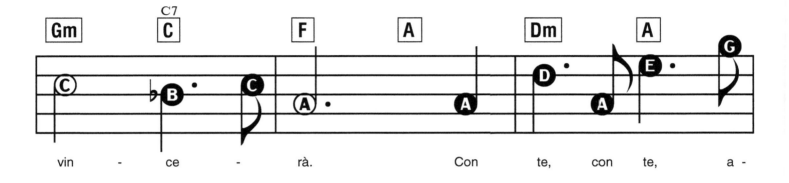

vin - ce - rà.   Con   te,   con   te,   a -

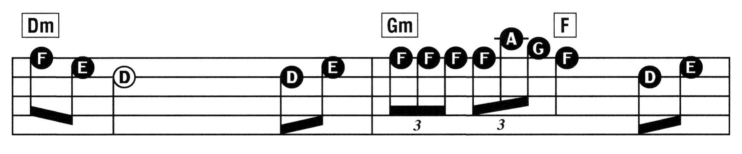

vrò. _____   Fa - rò   quel - lo che mi chie-de - rai   An - drò

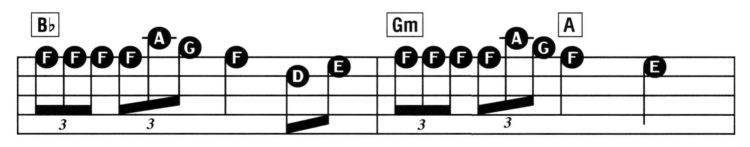

sem - pre do - vun - que tu an - drai.   Da - rò   tut - to l'a - mo - re che ho,   per

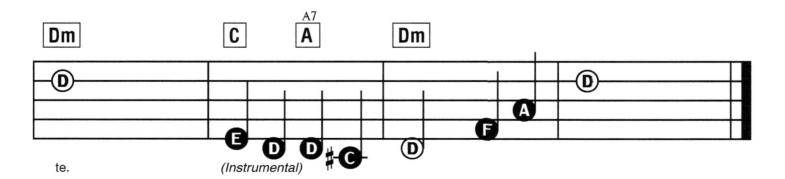

te.   *(Instrumental)*

The Prayer

Registration 8
Rhythm: 4/4 Ballad

Words and Music by Carole Bayer Sager
and David Foster

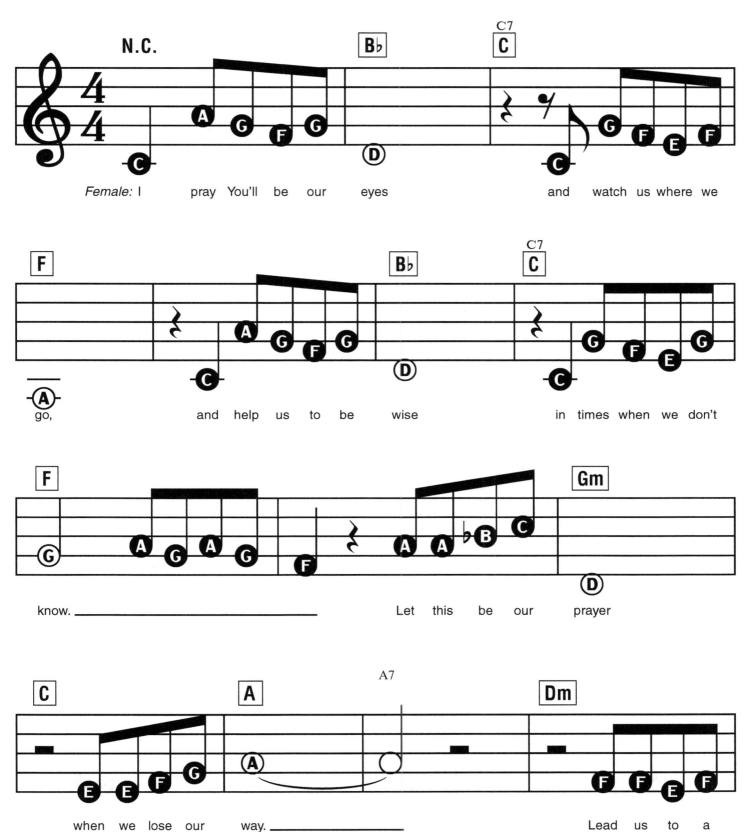

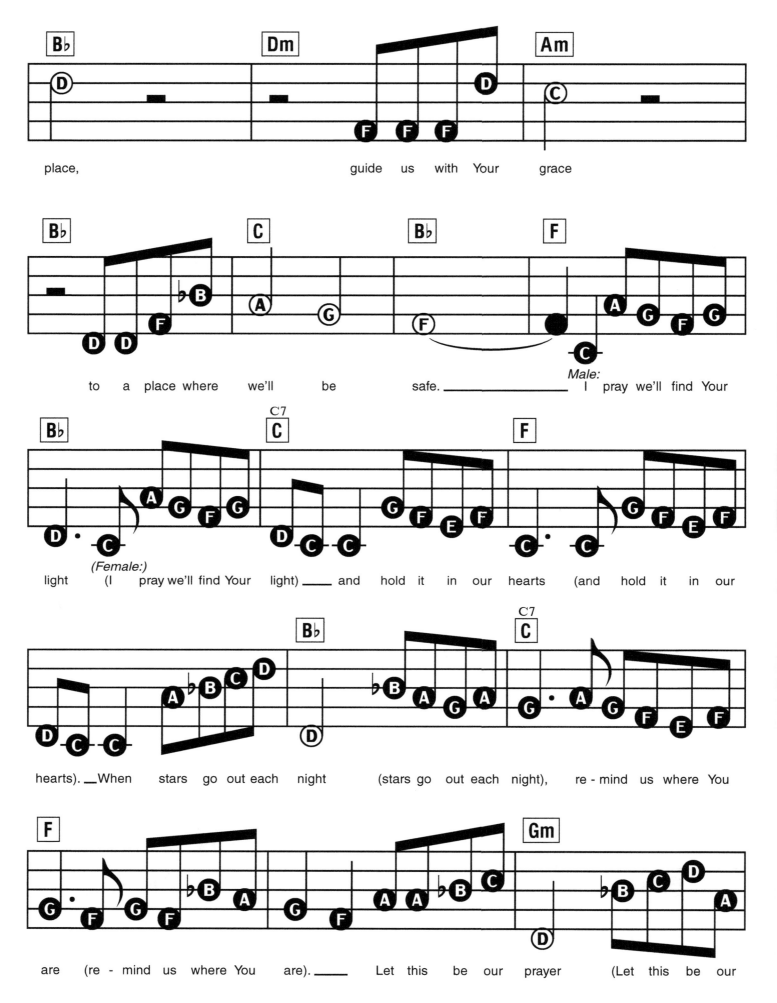

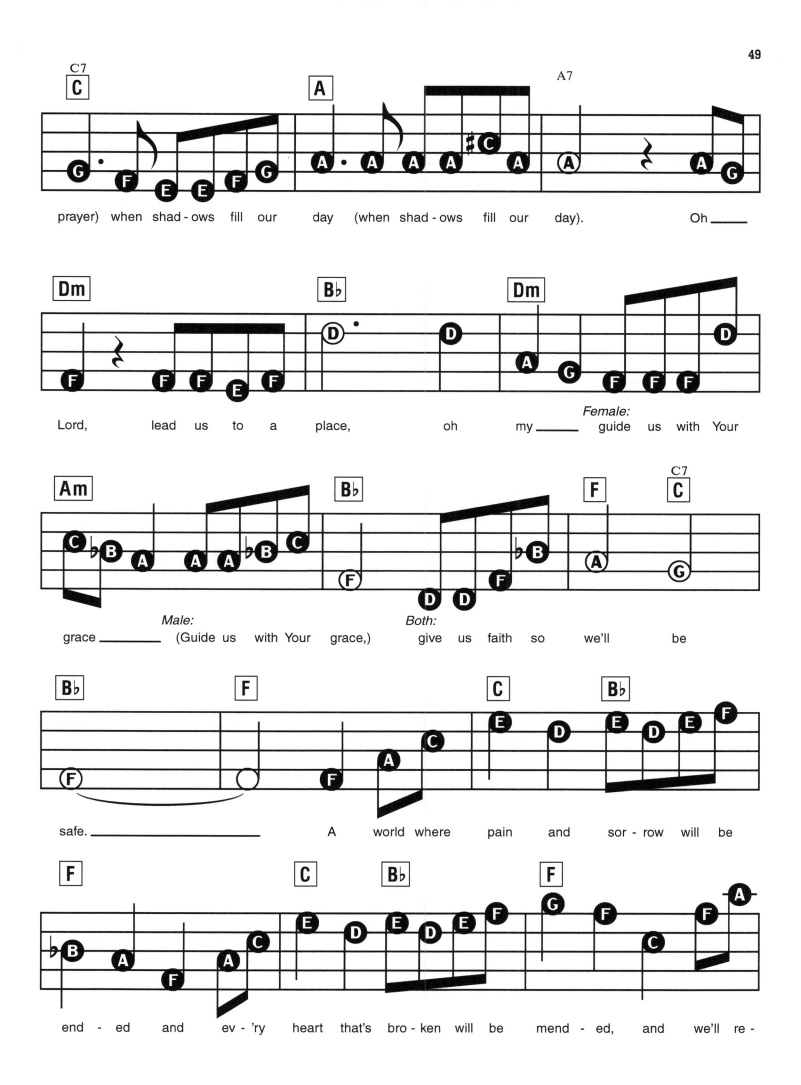

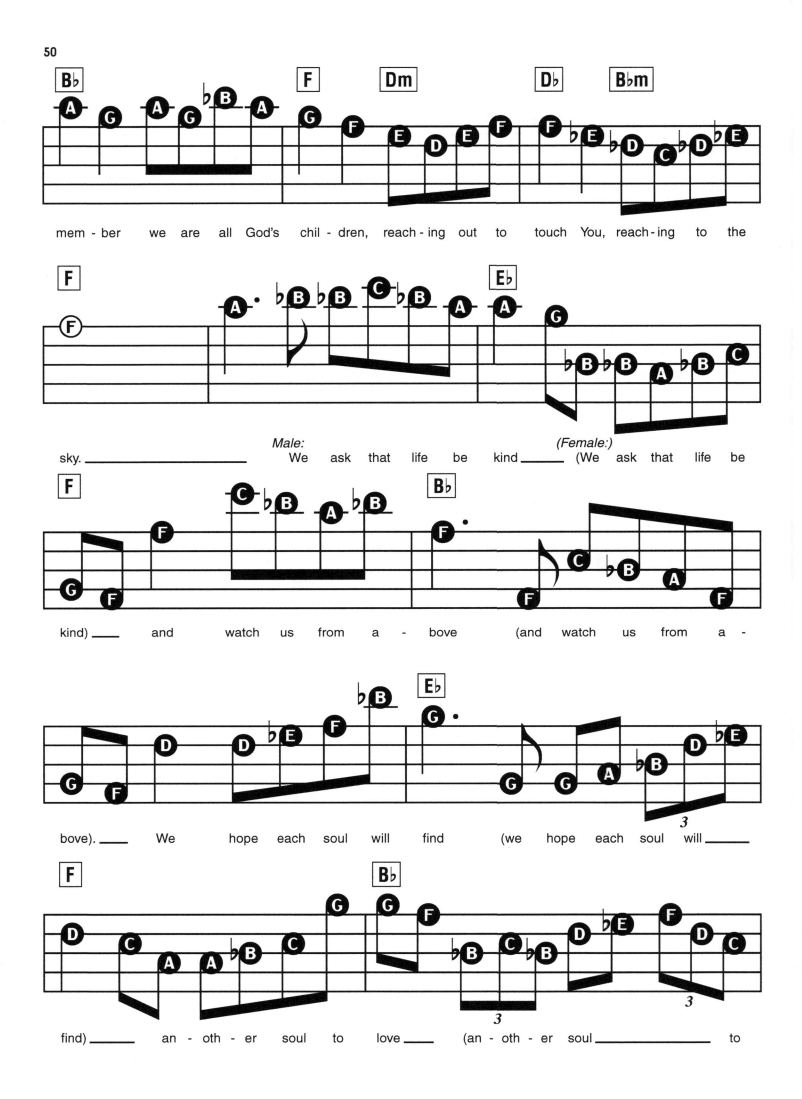

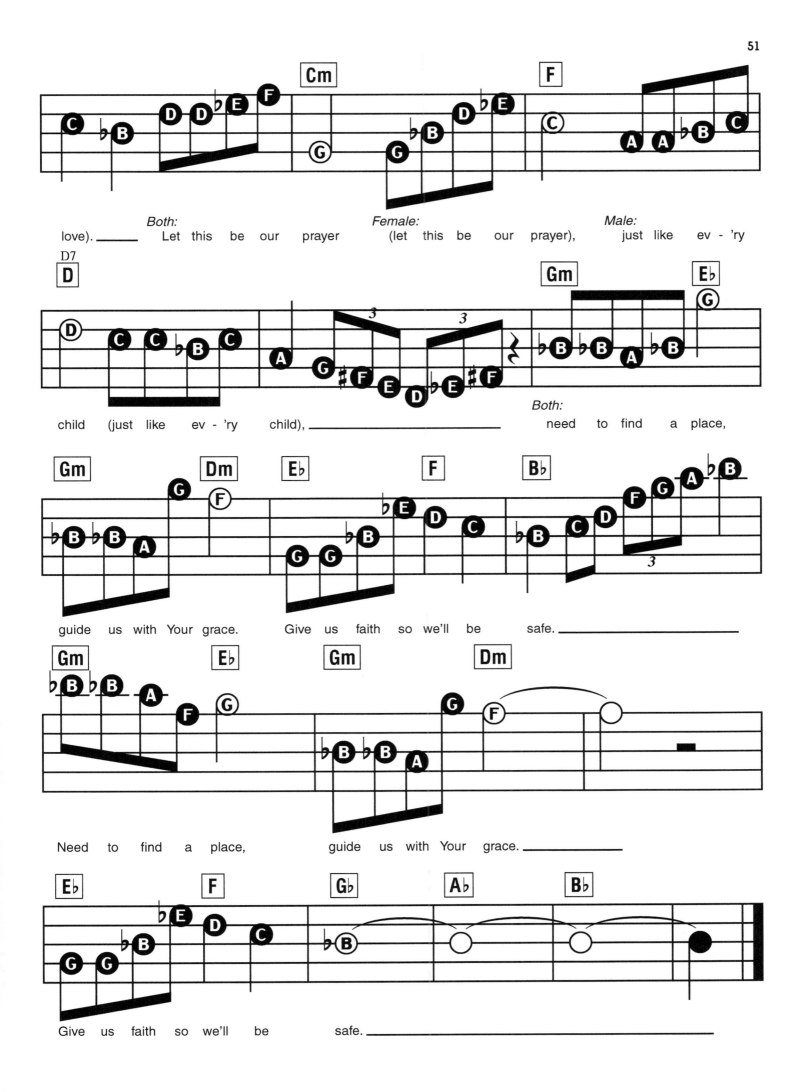

Remember When It Rained

Registration 8
Rhythm: 4/4 Ballad

Words and Music by Eric Mouquet
and Josh Groban

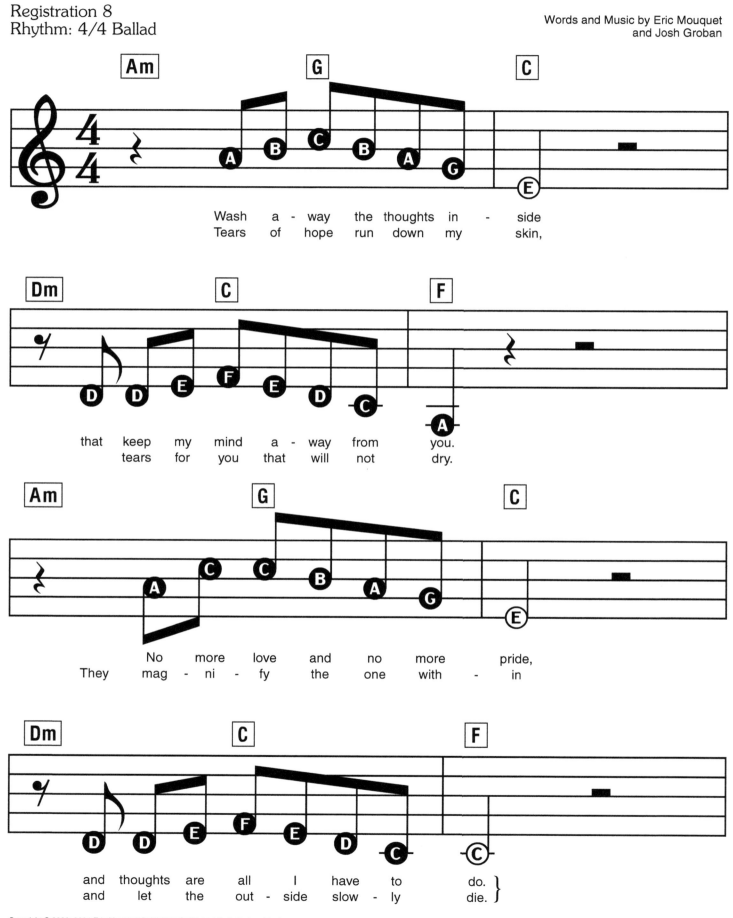

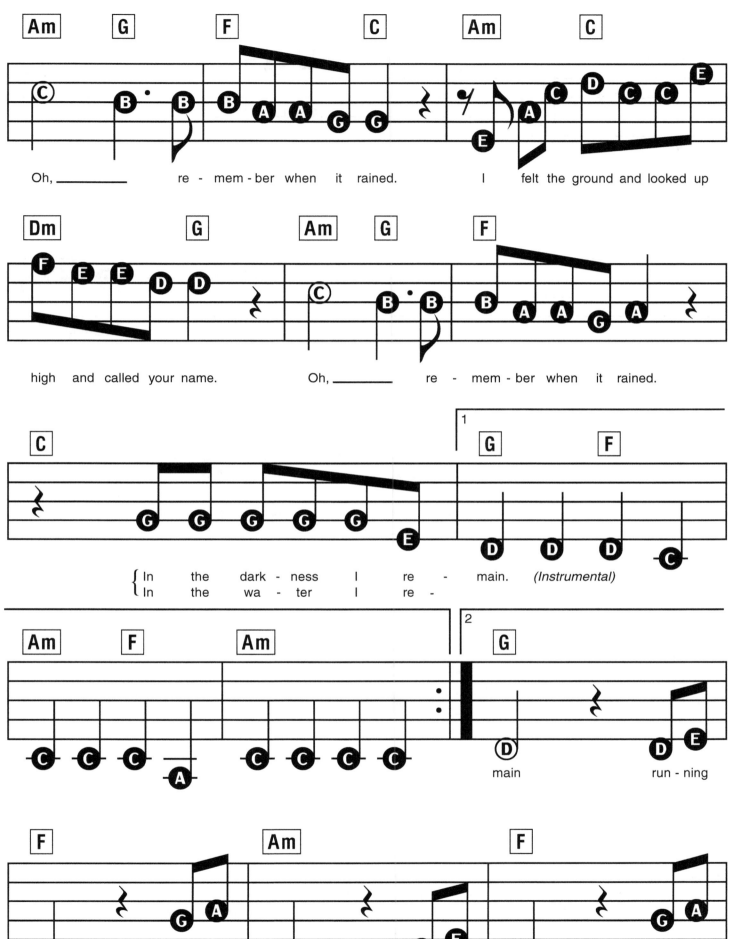

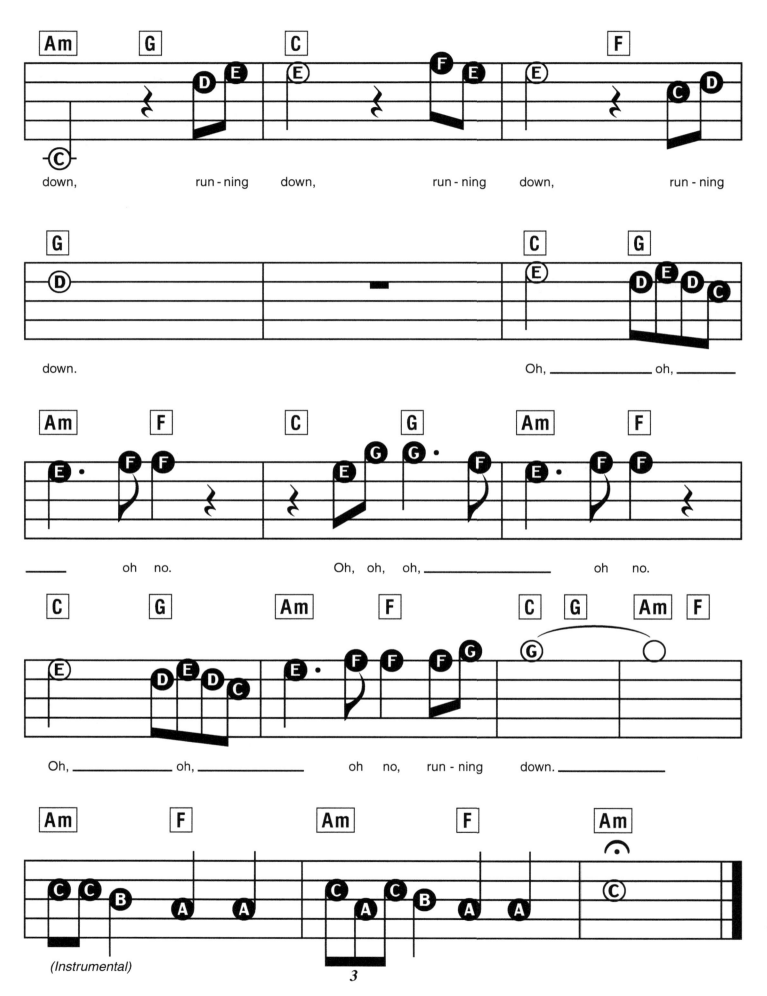

So She Dances

Registration 8
Rhythm: Waltz

Words and Music by Asher Lenz
and Adam Crossley

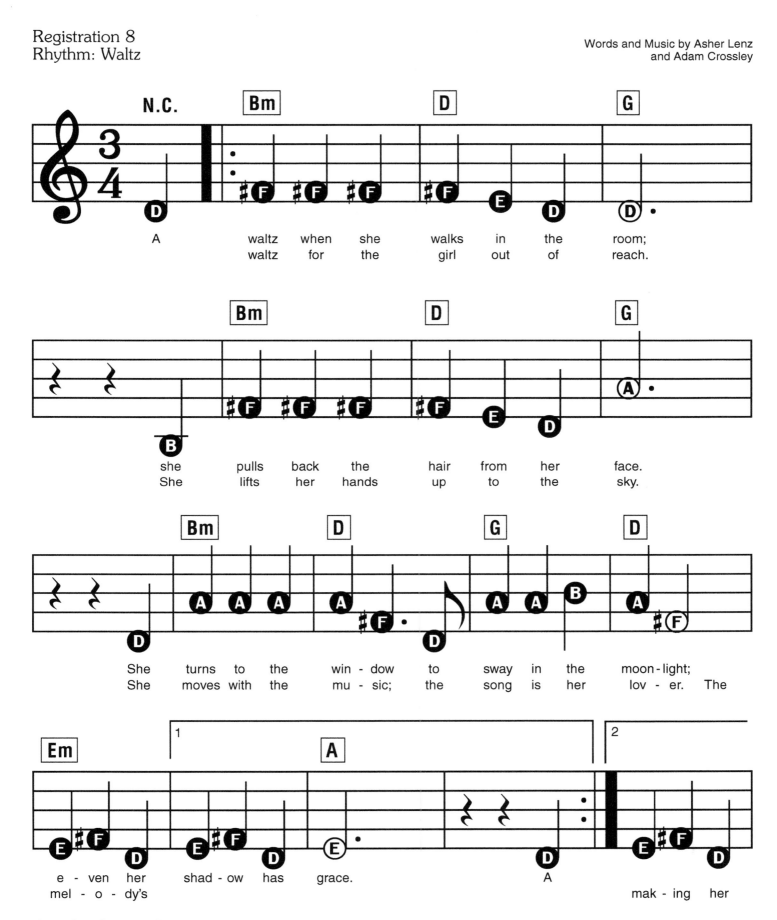

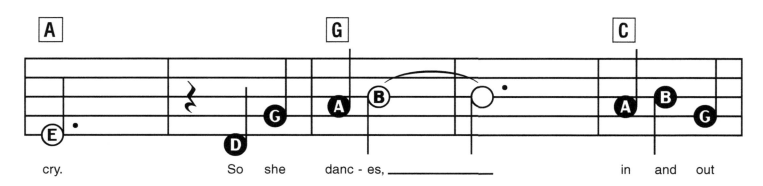

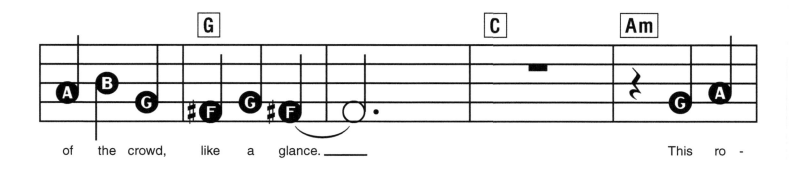

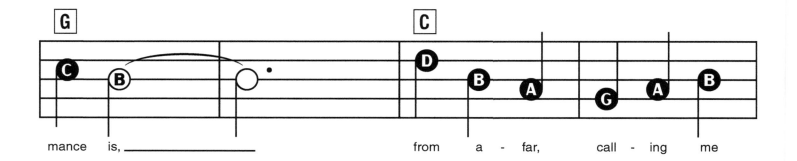

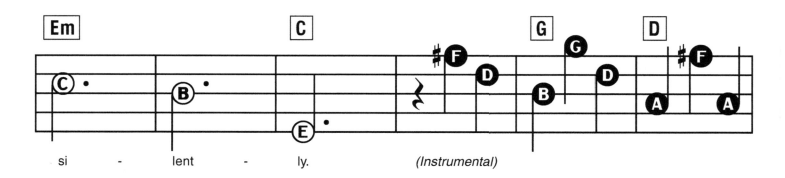

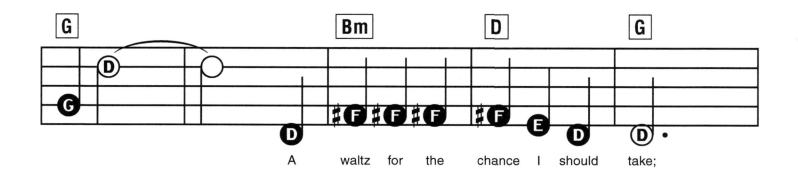

57

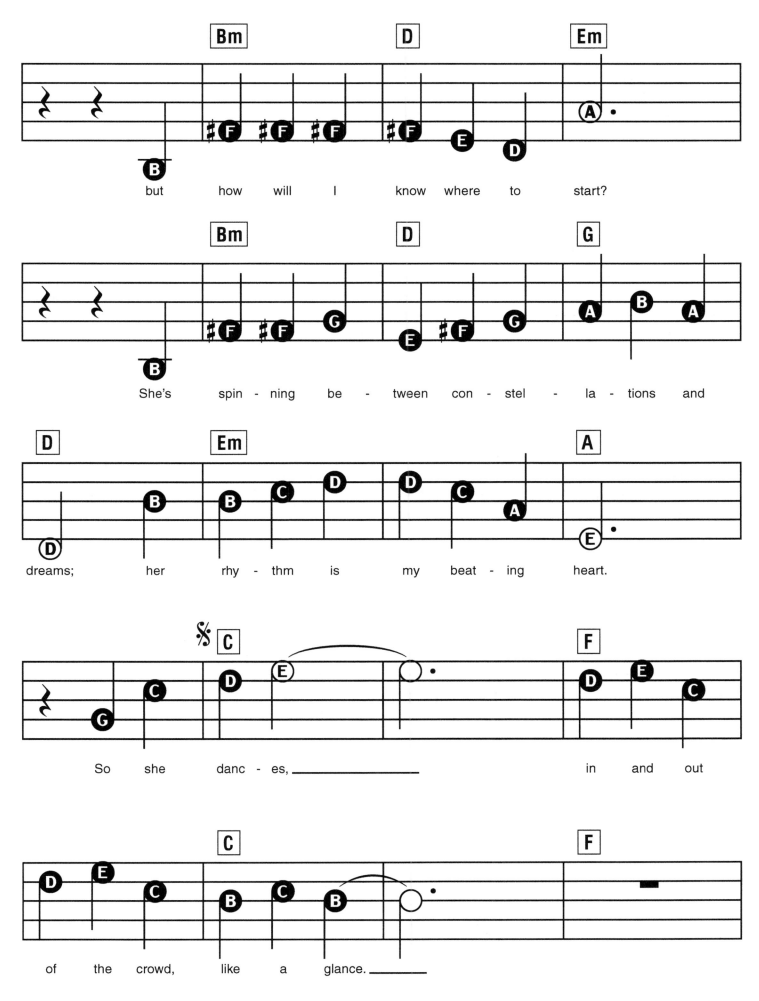

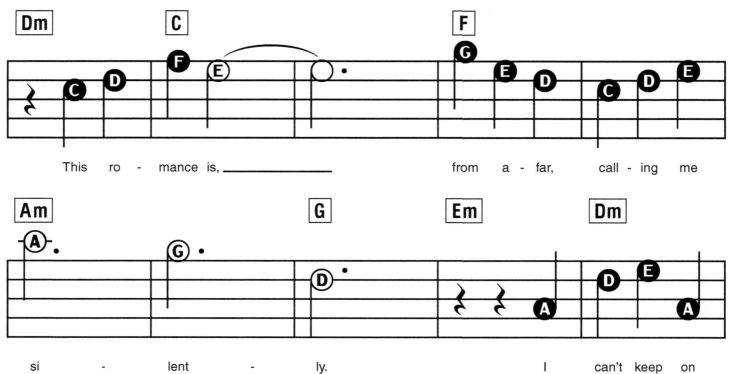

This ro - mance is, _____ from a - far, call - ing me

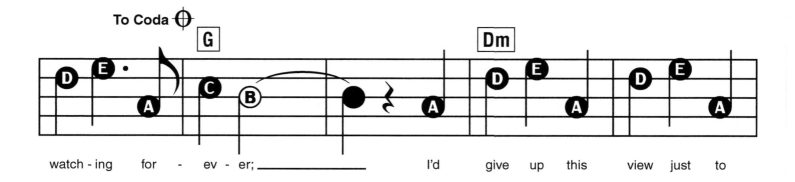

si - lent - ly. I can't keep on

To Coda ⊕

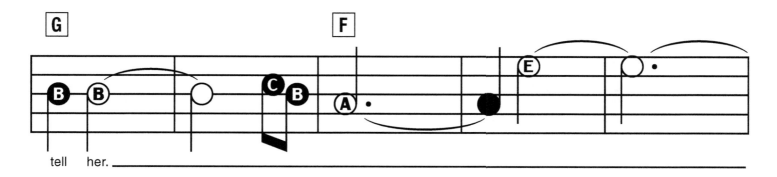

watch - ing for - ev - er; _____ I'd give up this view just to

tell her. _____

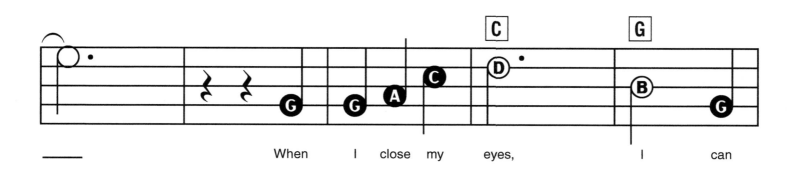

_____ When I close my eyes, I can

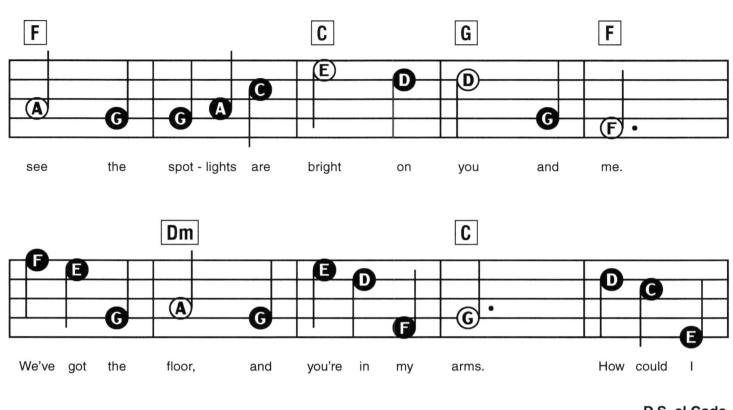

see   the   spot - lights are   bright   on   you   and   me.

We've got the floor, and you're in my arms.   How could I

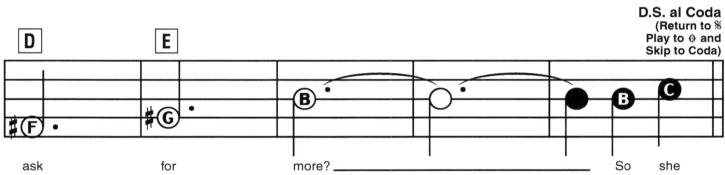

D.S. al Coda
(Return to %
Play to ⊕ and
Skip to Coda)

ask   for   more? _____ So she

CODA
⊕ G

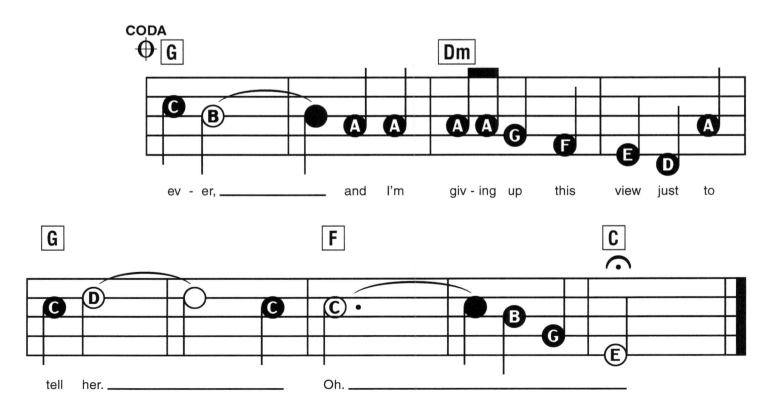

ev - er, _____ and I'm giv - ing up this view just to

tell her. _____ Oh. _____

To Where You Are

Registration 2
Rhythm: 4/4 Ballad

Words and Music by Linda Thompson
and Richard Marx

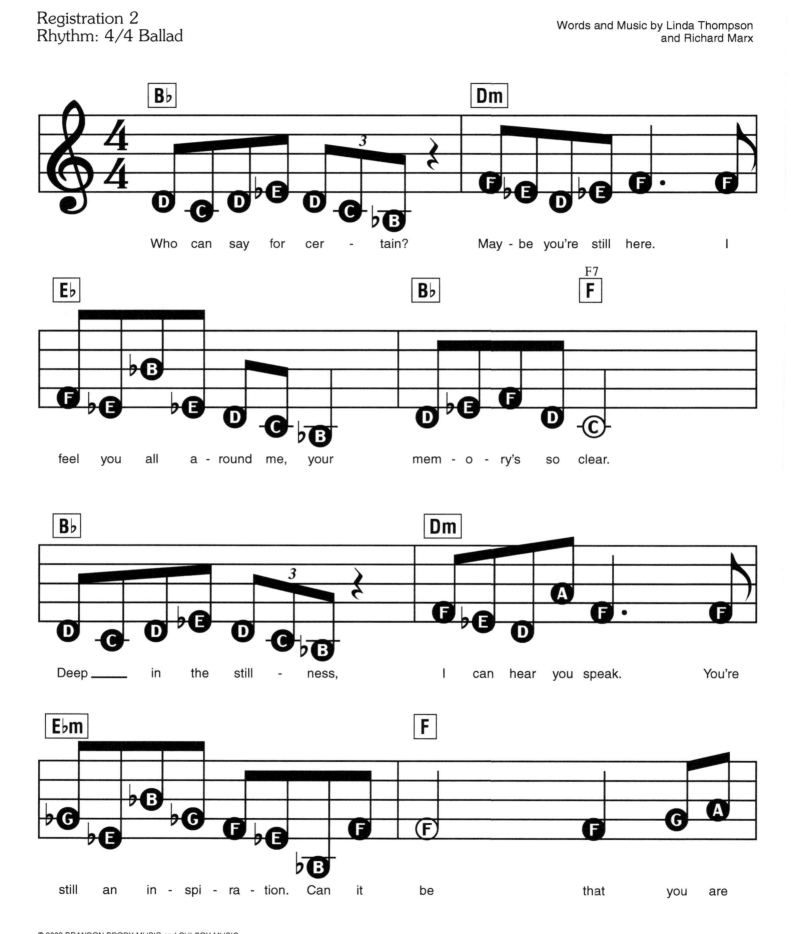

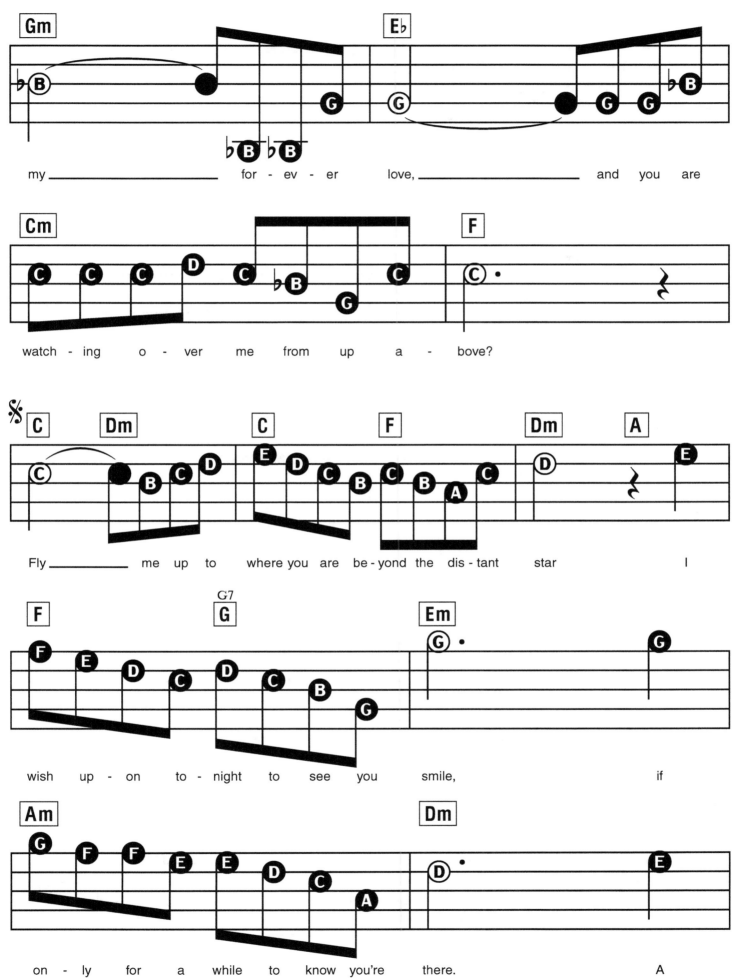

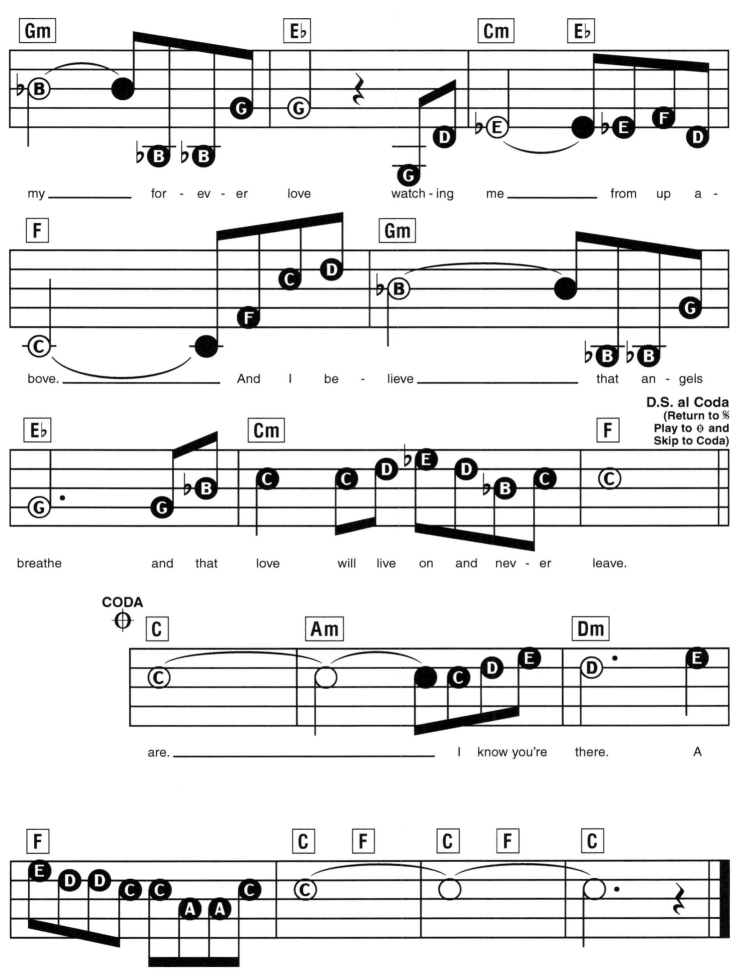

Un Dia Llegara

Registration 4
Rhythm: Waltz

Music by Oksana Grigorieva
Lyrics by Claudia Brant

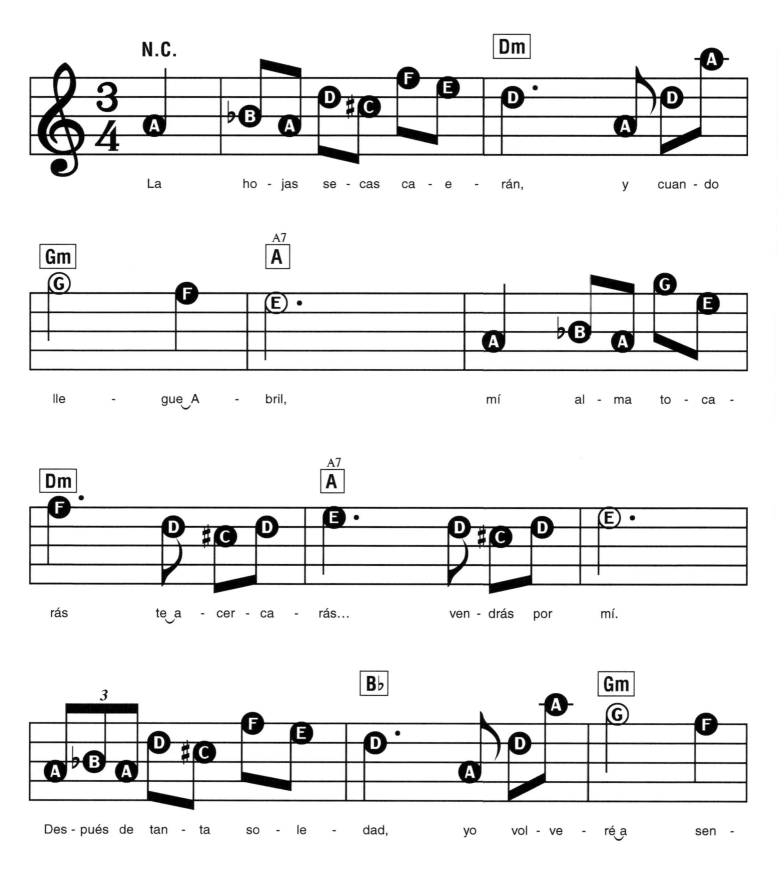

La ho - jas se - cas ca - e - rán, y cuan - do

lle - gue A - bril, mí al - ma to - ca -

rás te a - cer - ca - rás... ven - drás por mí.

Des - pués de tan - ta so - le - dad, yo vol - ve - ré a sen -

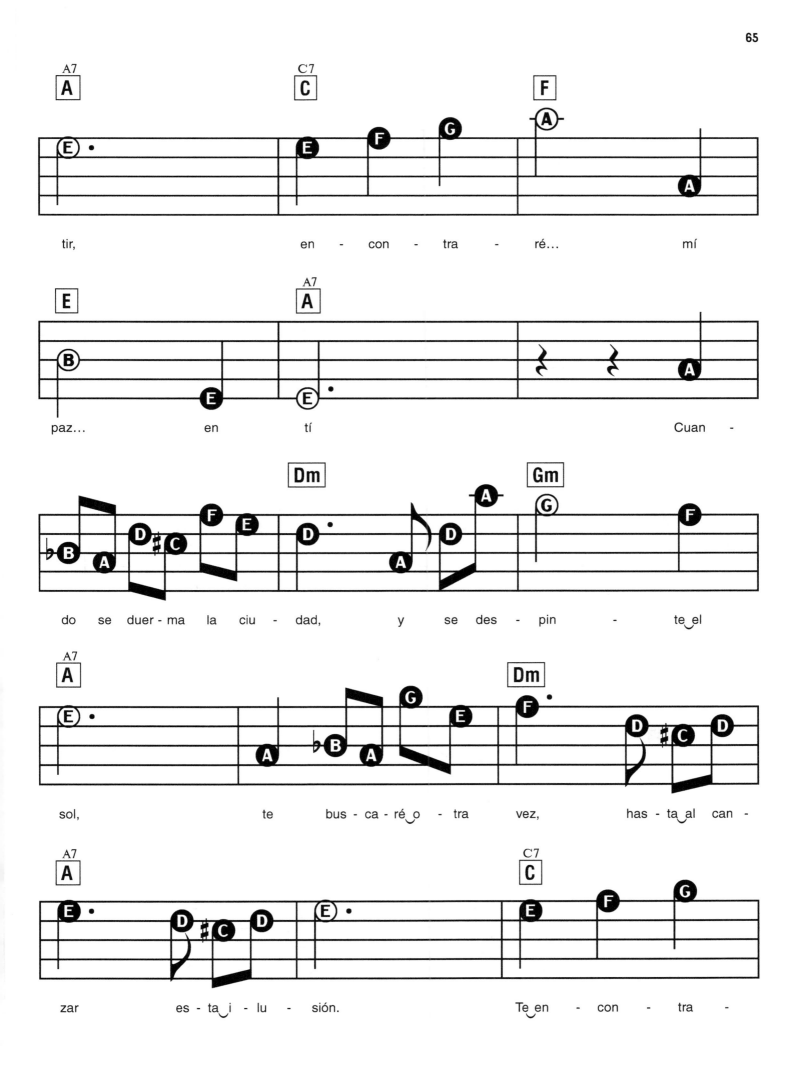

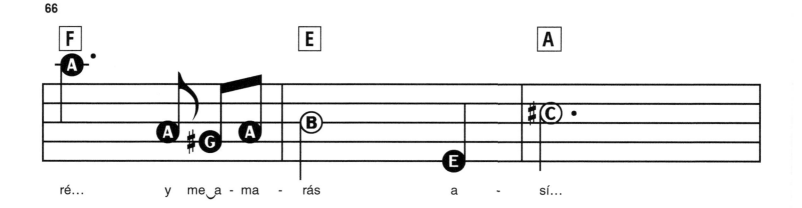

ré... y me a - ma - rás a - sí...

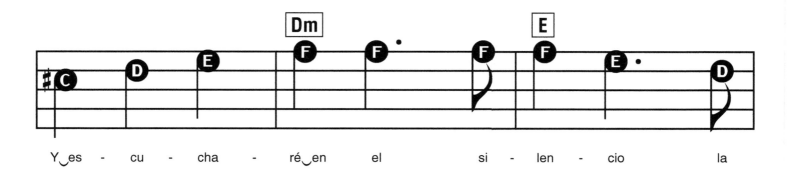

Y es - cu - cha - ré en el si - len - cio la

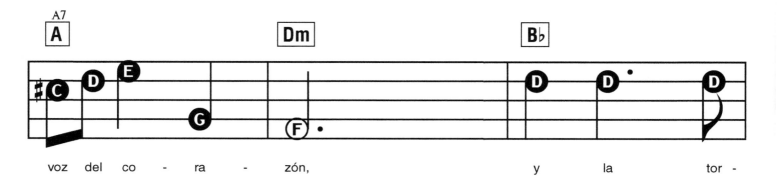

voz del co - ra - zón, y la tor -

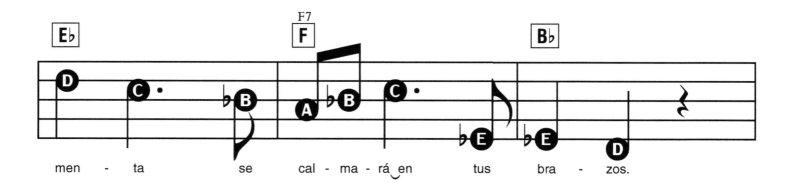

men - ta se cal - ma - rá en tus bra - zos.

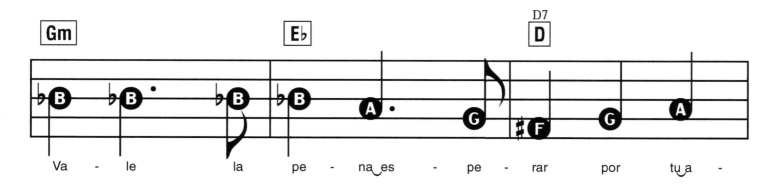

Va - le la pe - na es - pe - rar por tu a -

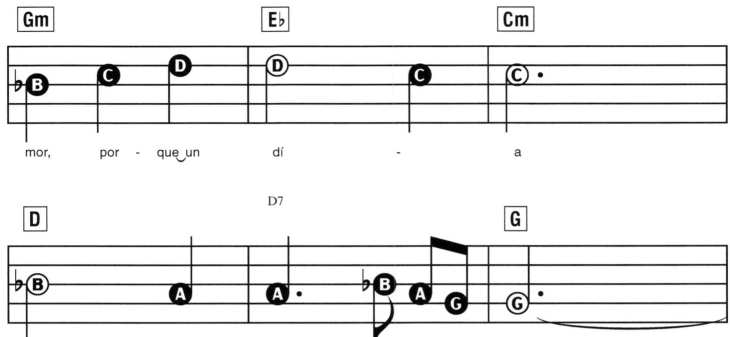

mor,   por - que_un   dí   -   a

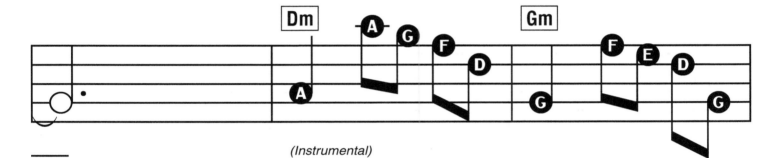

lle   -   ga   -   ras. _____

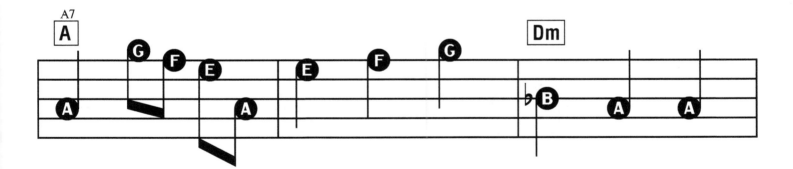

_____   (Instrumental)

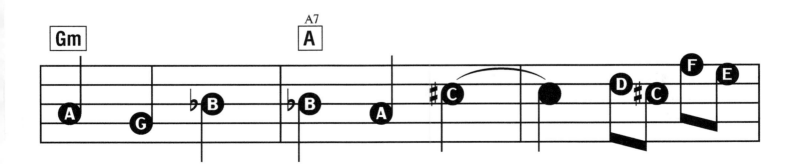

68

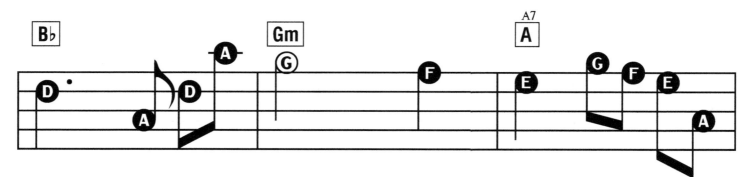

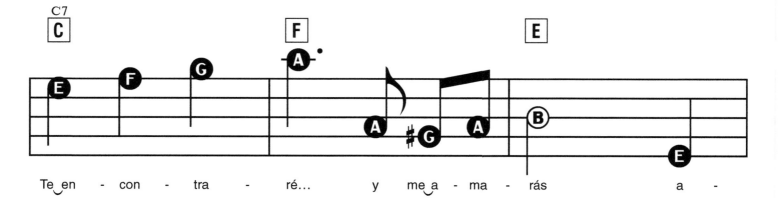

Te en - con - tra - ré... y me_a - ma - rás a -

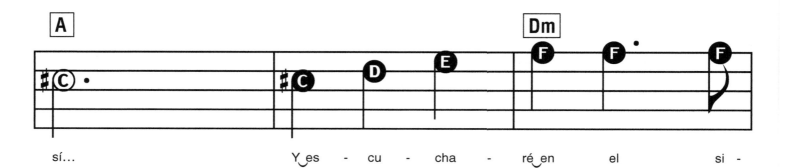

sí... Y_es - cu - cha - ré_en el si -

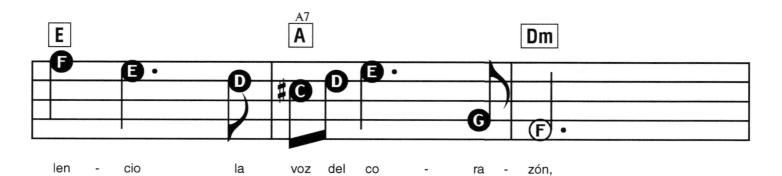

len - cio la voz del co - ra - zón,

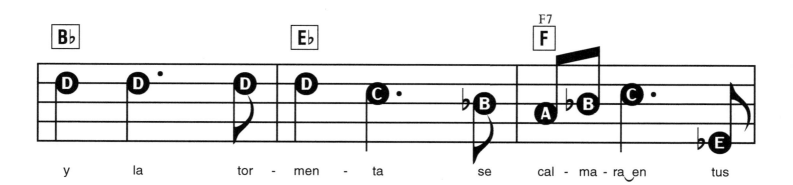

y la tor - men - ta se cal - ma - ra_en tus

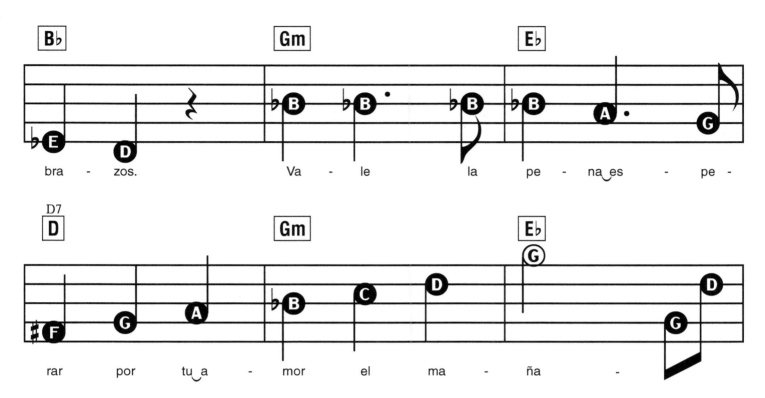

bra - zos.   Va - le   la   pe - na es - pe -

rar   por   tu a - mor   el   ma - ña -

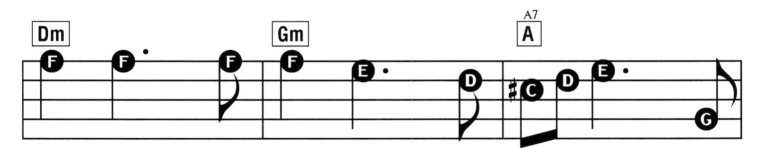

-     -   -

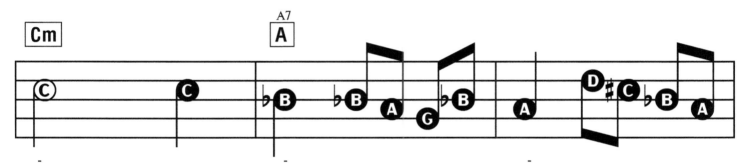

na...   *(Instrumental)*

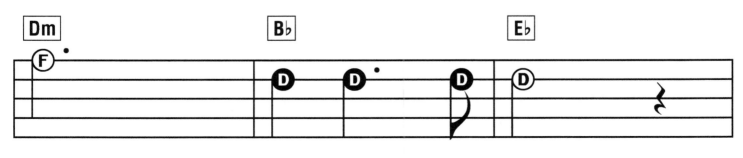

Te a - bra - za - ré...

70

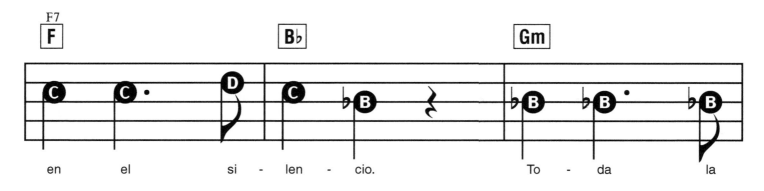

en el si - len - cio. To - da la

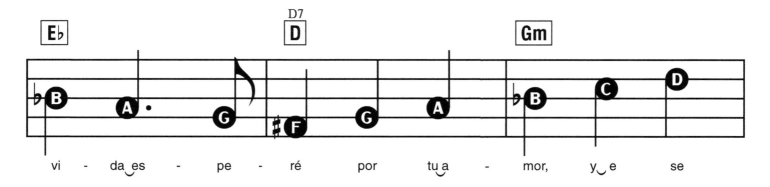

vi - da es - pe - ré por tu a - mor, y e se

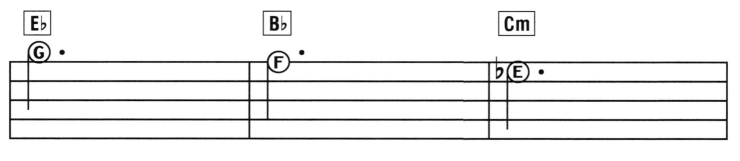

dí - a lle -

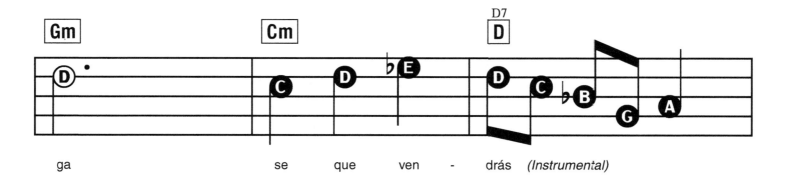

ga se que ven - drás *(Instrumental)*

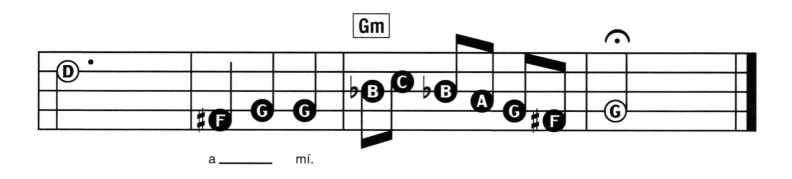

a _____ mí.

You Raise Me Up

Registration 3
Rhythm: Ballad

Words and Music by Brendan Graham
and Rolf Lovland

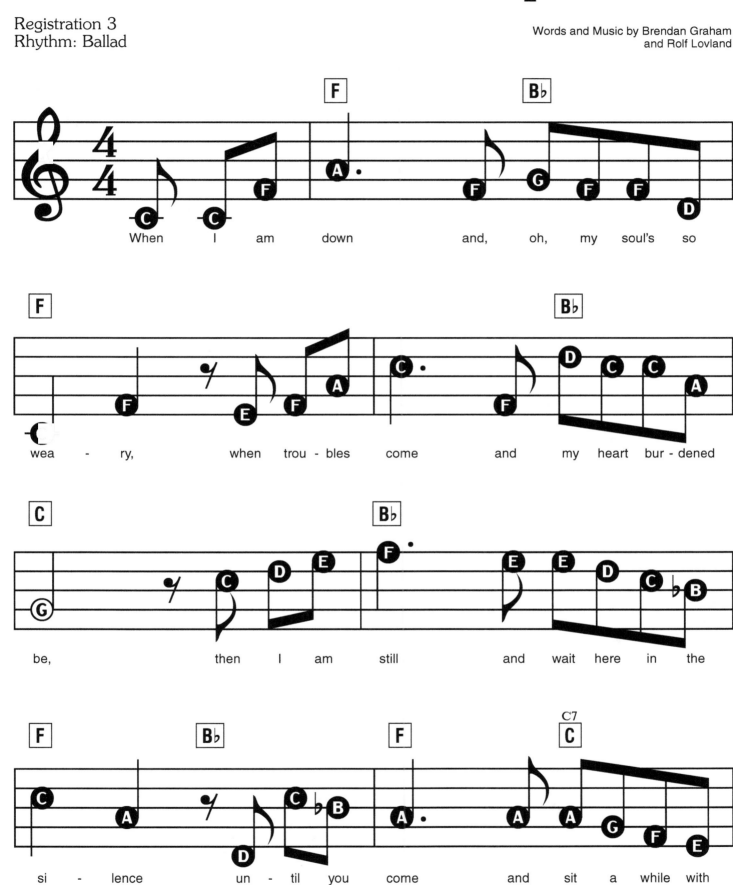

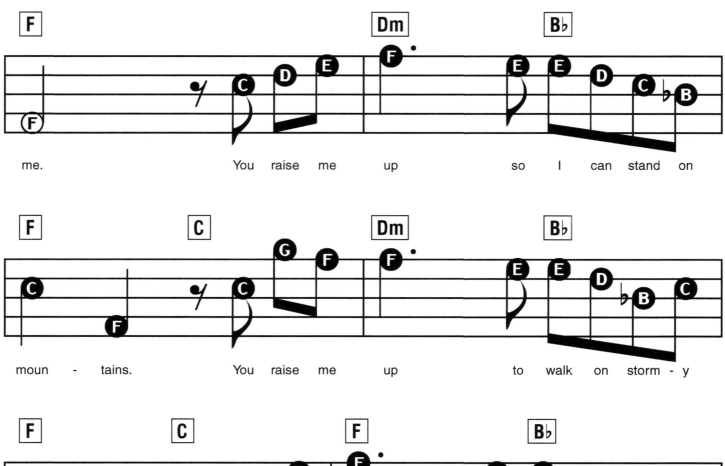

me.   You raise me   up   so I can stand on

moun - tains.   You raise me   up   to walk on storm - y

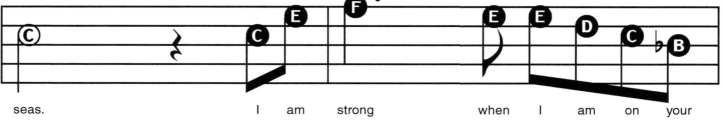

seas.   I am strong   when I am on your

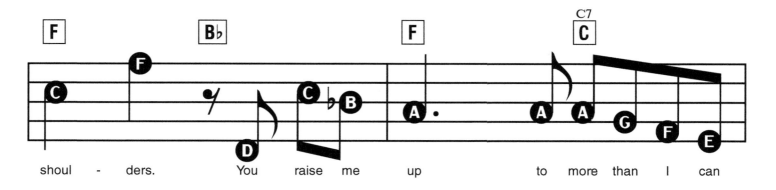

shoul - ders.   You raise me   up   to more than I can

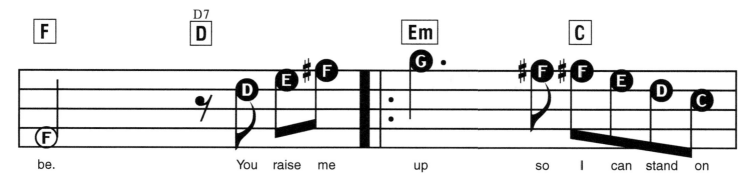

be.   You raise me   up   so I can stand on

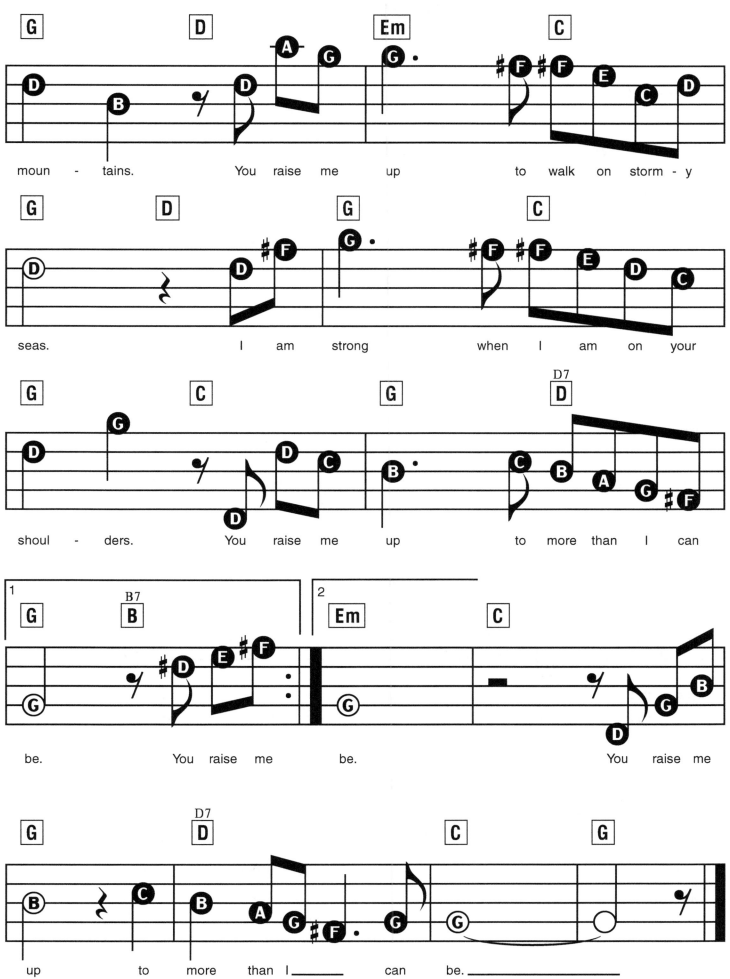

Vincent
(Starry, Starry Night)

Registration 7
Rhythm: 8 Beat or Pops

Words and Music by
Don McLean

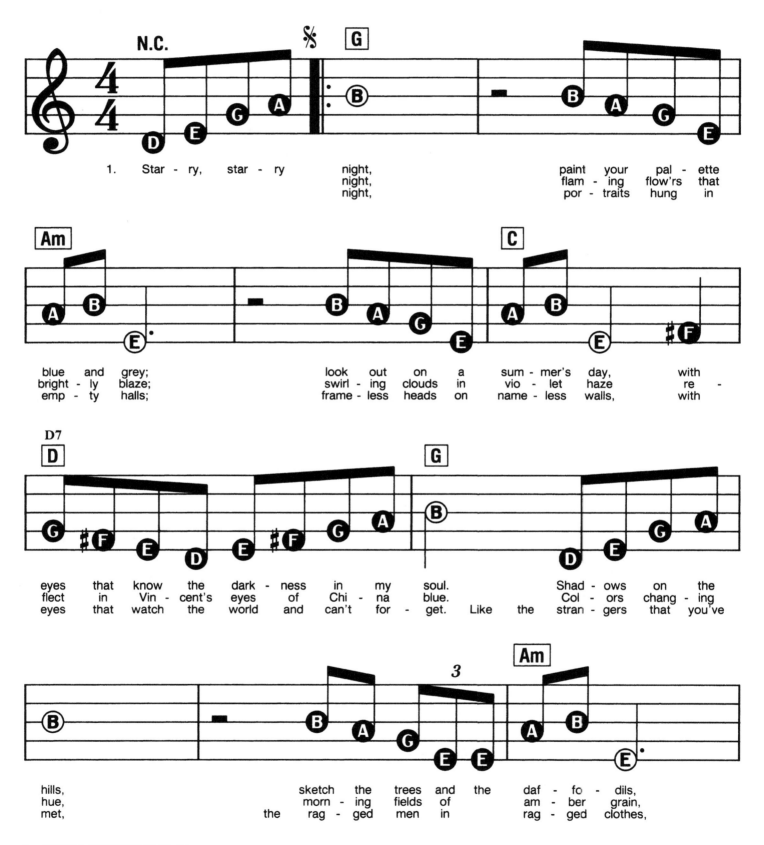

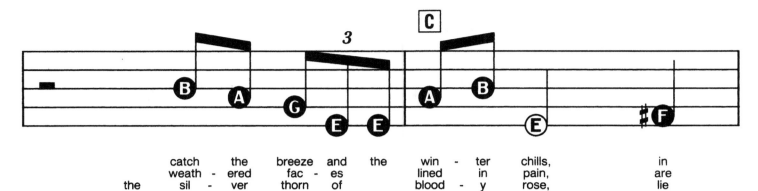

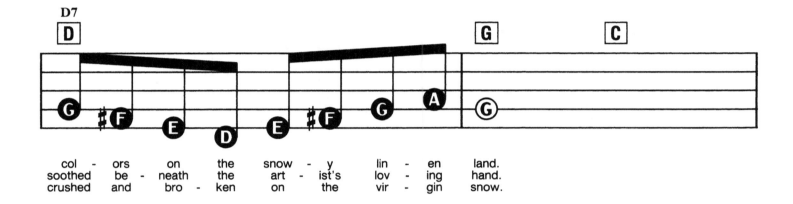

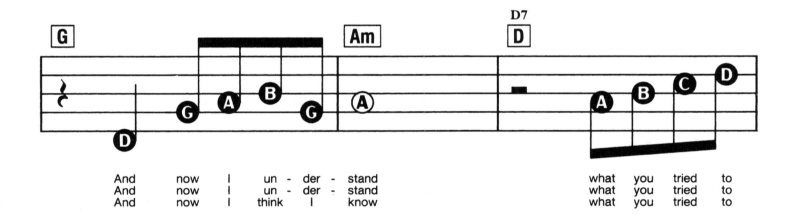

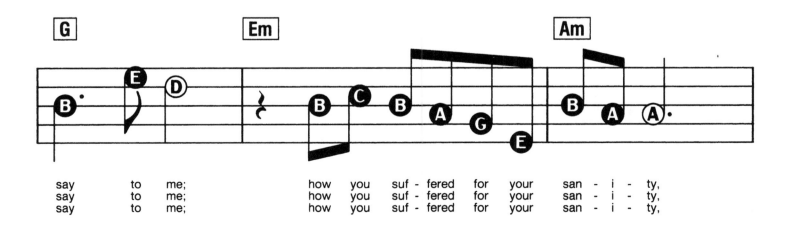

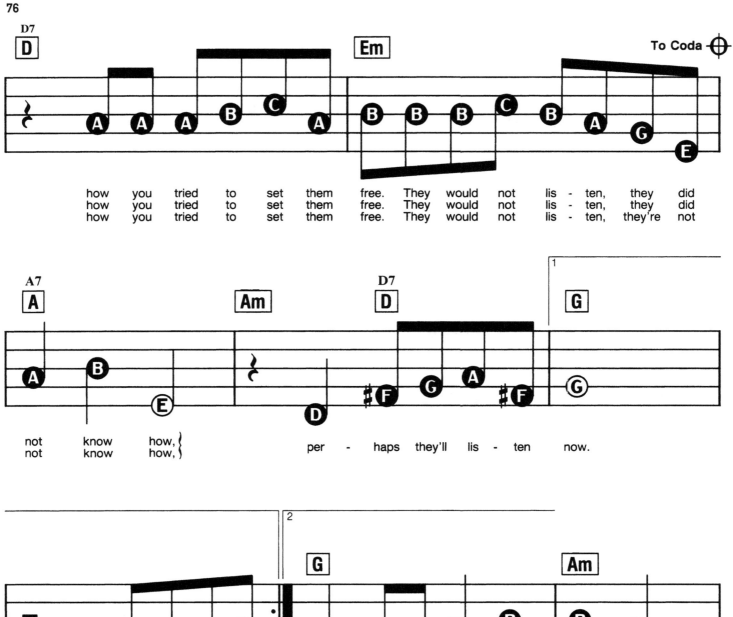

how   you   tried   to   set   them   free.   They   would   not   lis - ten,   they   did
how   you   tried   to   set   them   free.   They   would   not   lis - ten,   they   did
how   you   tried   to   set   them   free.   They   would   not   lis - ten,   they're   not

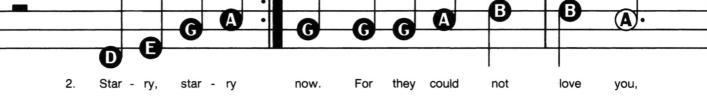

not   know   how,   {   per - haps   they'll   lis - ten   now.
not   know   how,   {

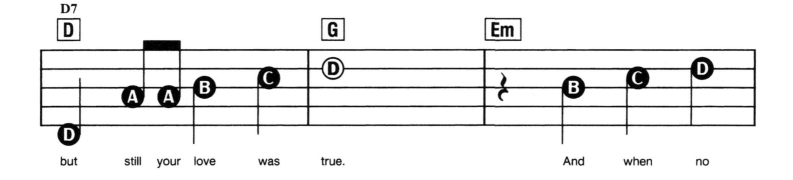

2.   Star - ry,   star - ry   now.   For   they   could   not   love   you,

but   still   your   love   was   true.   And   when   no

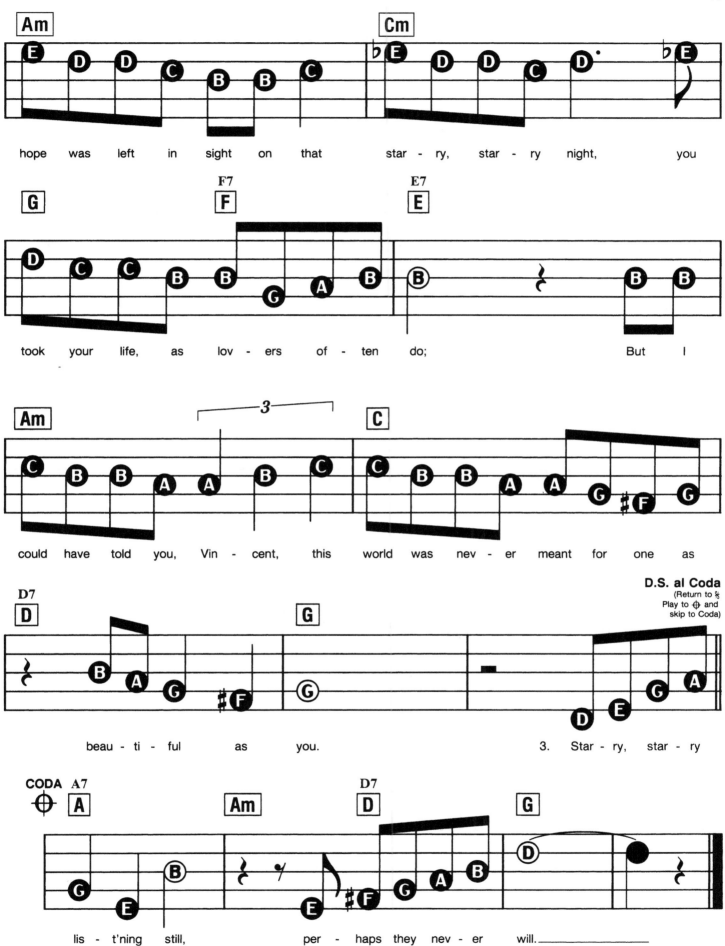

You Are Loved
(Don't Give Up)

Registration 7
Rhythm: 8 Beat or Rock

Words and Music by
Thomas Salter

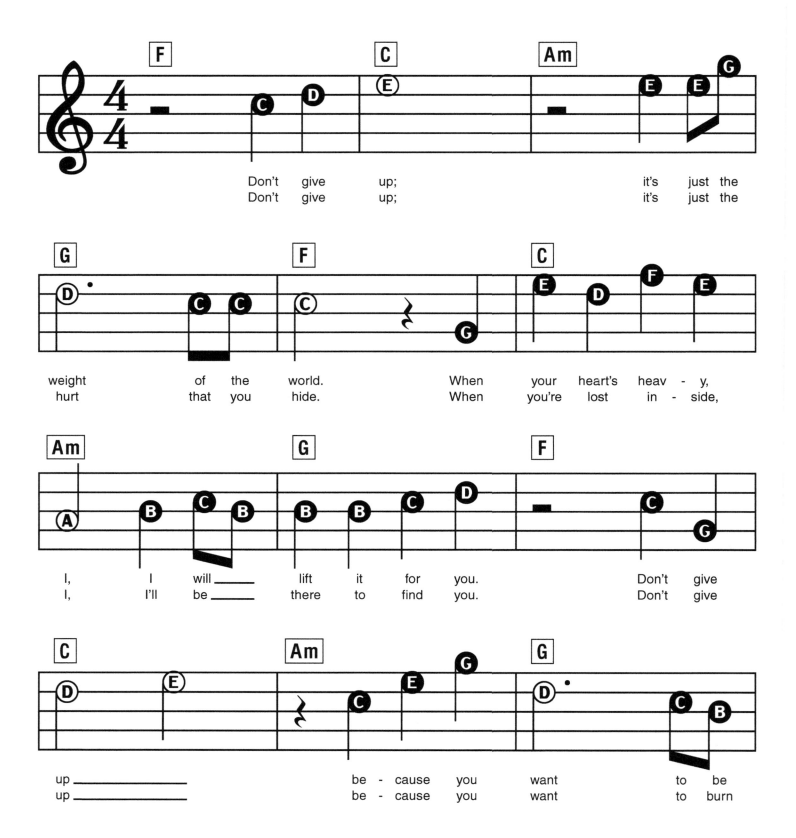

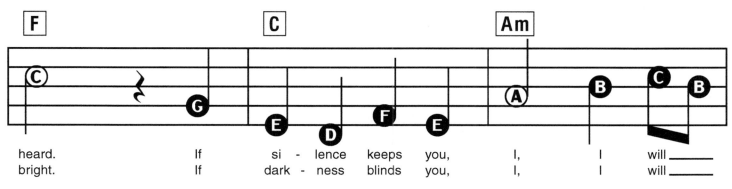

heard.   If   si - lence   keeps   you,   I,   I   will _____
bright.   If   dark - ness   blinds   you,   I,   I   will _____

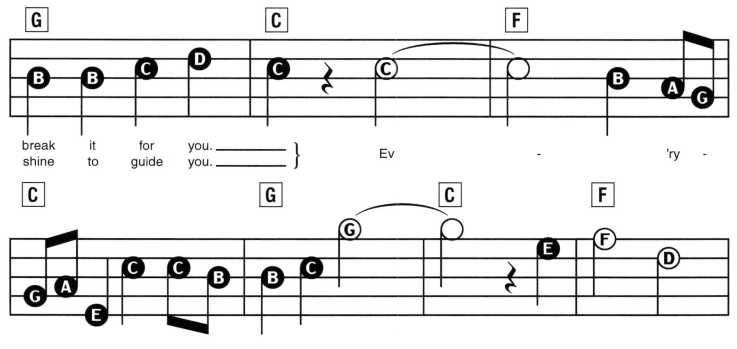

break   it   for   you. _____ }   Ev   -   'ry -
shine   to   guide   you. _____

bod - y   wants   to   be _____ un - der - stood; _____ well,   I   can

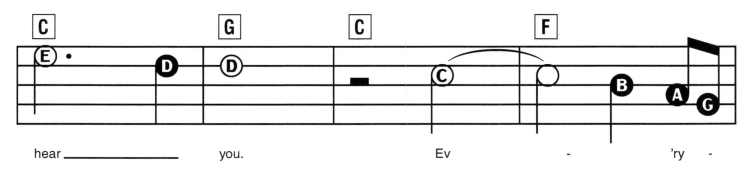

hear _____ you.   Ev   -   'ry -

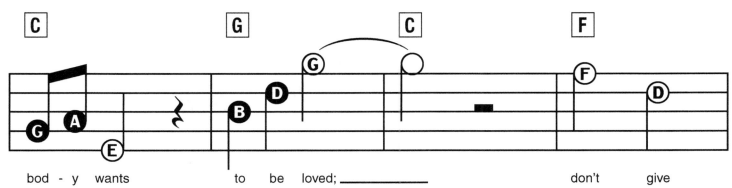

bod - y   wants   to   be   loved; _____ don't   give

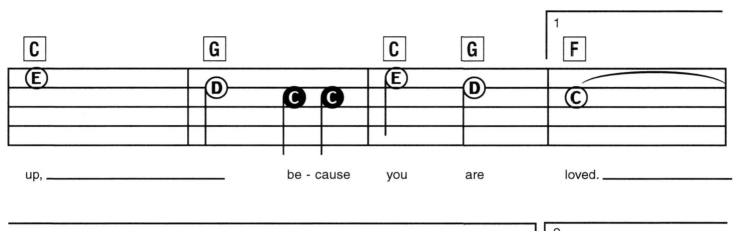

up, _____ be - cause you are loved. _____

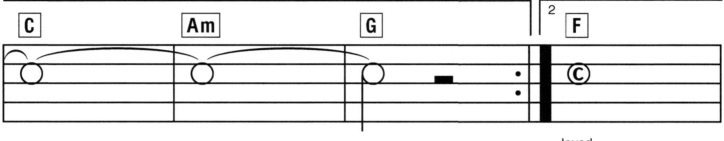

loved.

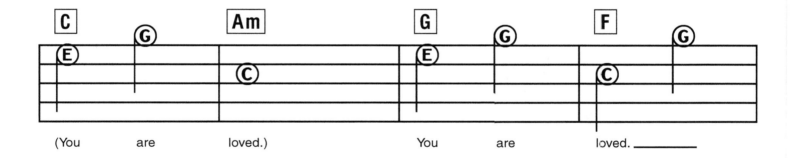

(You are loved.) You are loved. _____

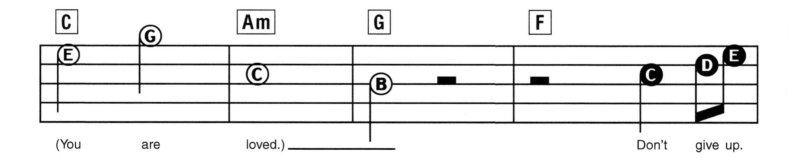

(You are loved.) _____ Don't give up.

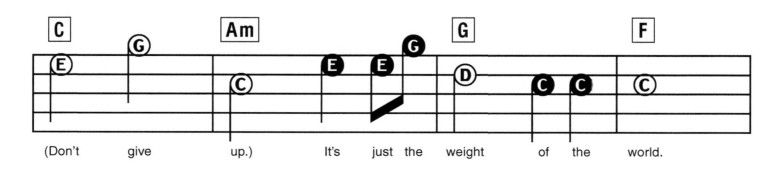

(Don't give up.) It's just the weight of the world.

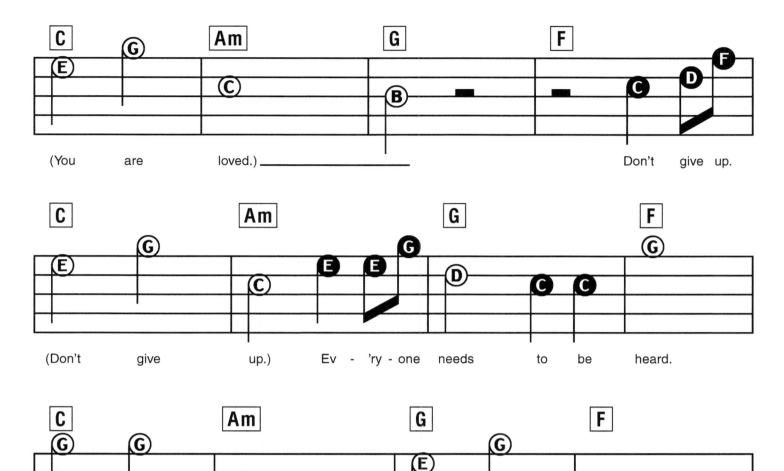

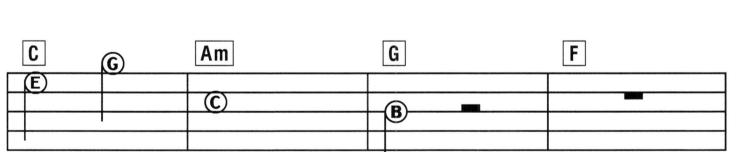

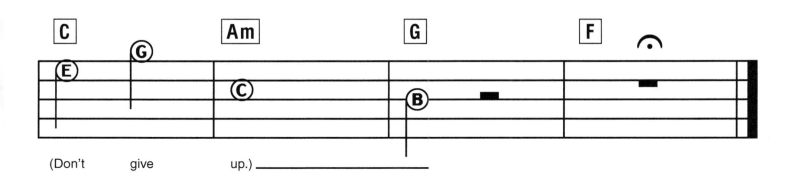

You're Still You

Registration 2
Rhythm: 4/4 Ballad

Words by Linda Thompson
Music by Ennio Morricone

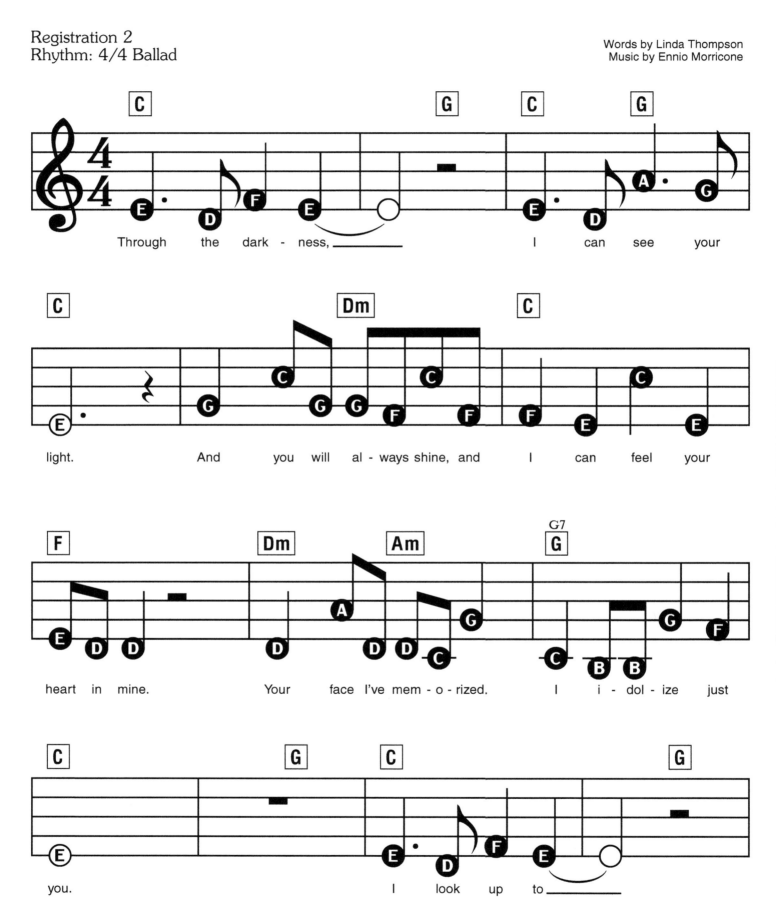

84

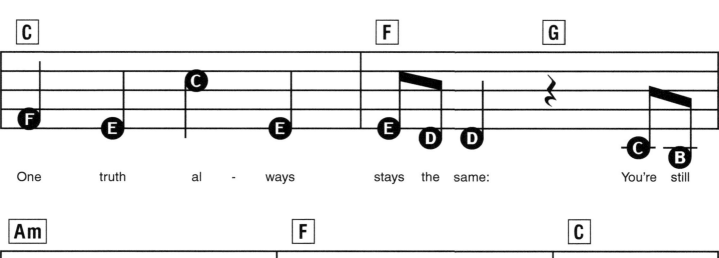

One truth al - ways stays the same: You're still

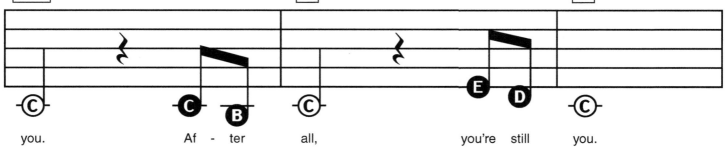

you. Af - ter all, you're still you.

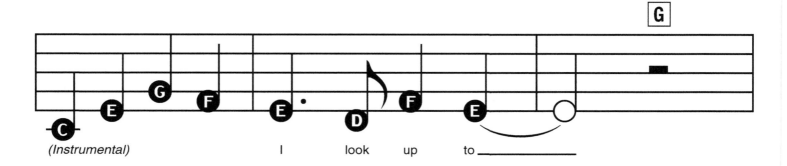

(Instrumental) I look up to _____

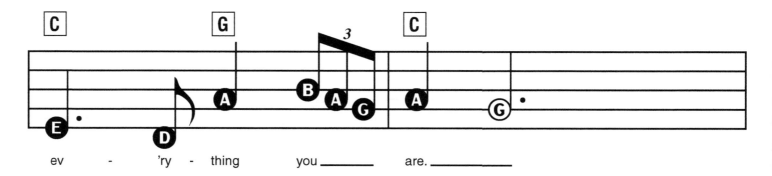

ev - 'ry - thing you _____ are. _____

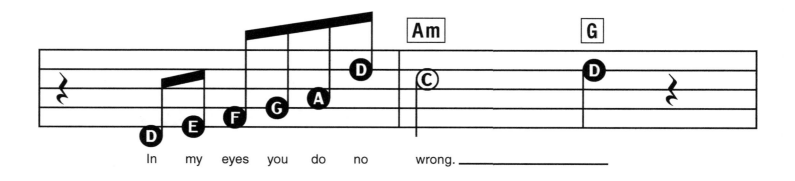

In my eyes you do no wrong. _____

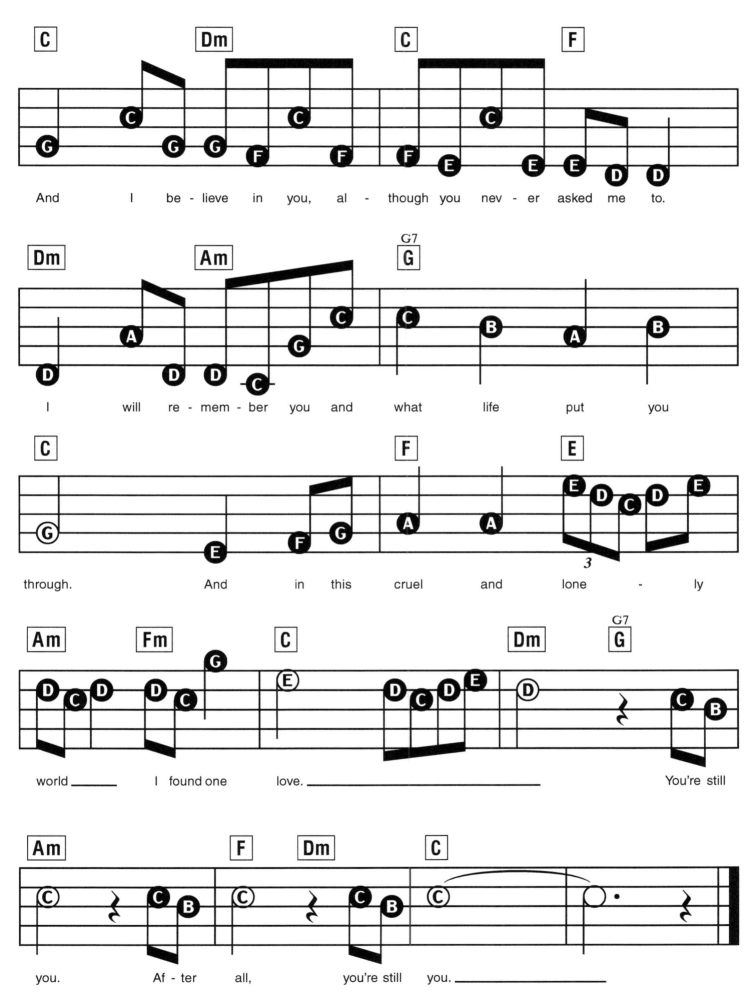

Registration Guide

- Match the Registration number on the song to the corresponding numbered category below. Select and activate an instrumental sound available on your instrument.

- Choose an automatic rhythm appropriate to the mood and style of the song. (Consult your Owner's Guide for proper operation of automatic rhythm features.)

- Adjust the tempo and volume controls to comfortable settings.

Registration

1	Mellow	Flutes, Clarinet, Oboe, Flugel Horn, Trombone, French Horn, Organ Flutes
2	Ensemble	Brass Section, Sax Section, Wind Ensemble, Full Organ, Theater Organ
3	Strings	Violin, Viola, Cello, Fiddle, String Ensemble, Pizzicato, Organ Strings
4	Guitars	Acoustic/Electric Guitars, Banjo, Mandolin, Dulcimer, Ukulele, Hawaiian Guitar
5	Mallets	Vibraphone, Marimba, Xylophone, Steel Drums, Bells, Celesta, Chimes
6	Liturgical	Pipe Organ, Hand Bells, Vocal Ensemble, Choir, Organ Flutes
7	Bright	Saxophones, Trumpet, Mute Trumpet, Synth Leads, Jazz/Gospel Organs
8	Piano	Piano, Electric Piano, Honky Tonk Piano, Harpsichord, Clavi
9	Novelty	Melodic Percussion, Wah Trumpet, Synth, Whistle, Kazoo, Perc. Organ
10	Bellows	Accordion, French Accordion, Mussette, Harmonica, Pump Organ, Bagpipes